the 50 BEST ETHICAL STOCKS for CANADIANS

2001 edition

Deb Abbey and **Michael Jantzi**

MACMILLAN CANADA
TORONTO

First published in Canada in 2000 by
Macmillan Canada, an imprint of CDG Books Canada

Canadian Cataloguing in Publication Data

Abbey, Deb
    The 50 best ethical stocks for Canadians

Includes index.

ISBN 0-7715-7695-1

1. Investments — Moral and ethical aspects — Canada. 2. Stocks — Canada. 3. Social responsibility of business — Canada. I. Jantzi, Michael. II. Title. III. Title: Fifty best ethical stocks for Canadians.
HD5152.A22 2001   332.63'22'0971   C00-932669-3

This book is available at special discounts for bulk purchases by your group or organization for sales promotions, premiums, fundraising and seminars. For details, contact: CDG Books Canada Inc., 99 Yorkville Avenue, Suite 400, Toronto, ON M5R 3K5. Tel: 416-963-8830. Toll Free: 1-877-963-8830. Fax: 416-923-4821. Web site: cdgbooks.com.

1 2 3 4 5 TRANS-B-G 04 03 02 01 00

Cover & text design: Kyle Gell art and design

Macmillan Canada
An imprint of CDG Books Canada Inc.
Toronto

Printed in Canada    Text pages printed on recycled paper.

For Perry, Brooke, and Brenna
– D.A.

For Amy and Valerie
– M.J.

CONTENTS

ACKNOWLEDGMENTS

The job of researching and writing a book such as this is too daunting for two people to tackle alone. Fortunately, we had a wealth of expertise upon which to draw. The team at Michael Jantzi Research Associates Inc. (MJRA) in Toronto provided the bulk of the social and environmental research, especially for the Canadian and European stocks. Kevin Ranney and Robert Gross at MJRA deserve special mention. We also wish to acknowledge the efforts of Steve Lydenberg and his team at Kinder, Lydenberg, Domini & Co., Inc. in Boston whose social and environmental research on U.S. equities was invaluable. MJRA's partners in the SIRI Group, primarily Swedish-based CaringCompany AB, provided some research on the European stocks as well.

We relied on the capable hands of Perry Abbey and his team at United Capital Securities to help piece together the financial picture for each of stocks profiled. We would be remiss if we didn't thank our family and friends for their love and encouragement during this project. Joel Solomon at Renewal Partners also deserves our thanks for his unwavering support of the work we do. Finally, we owe a debt of gratitude to the people at CDG Books, whose professionalism was in evidence every step of the way.

Deb Abbey
Michael Jantzi

INTRODUCTION

What Is Social Investing?

When we chose the title of this book we were reluctant to use the word *ethical*. Ethical implies a kind of moral high ground and the 50 companies that we've chosen, like many others, are simply trying to be profitable while being as socially responsible as possible.

In North America, making investment decisions that integrate your personal values, your concerns for society, and your financial needs is commonly known as *socially responsible investing* or *social investing*. Using the term *social* alludes to the interdependence of human beings living together in communities. Recognizing that we all depend on each other moves us one step closer to solving some of the world's problems.

It should come as no surprise that social investing has its roots in the turbulent 1960s. In 1962 Rachel Carson wrote *Silent Spring* and North Americans digested the implications of corporate environmental performance (and a few parts per million of DDT). Civil rights, women's liberation, labour rights, and the war in Southeast Asia fuelled more than a decade of increasing awareness and protest. In the late 1970s international attention focused on apartheid in South Africa, and social investors refused to invest in companies that did business there and sponsored shareholder resolutions urging companies to withdraw from South Africa.

In subsequent decades, significant environmental incidents like Bhopal and Exxon *Valdez* and human rights abuses in countries like Nigeria, Burma, and the Sudan have continued to draw attention to the devastating results of not paying attention to the behaviour of corporations at home and abroad.

Social investors are part of an emerging group of conscious consumers that American sociologist Paul Ray calls "Cultural Creatives."
If U.S. statistics are any guide, they comprise 25 percent of the population, at least 60 percent of them are women, they're well-educated,
they're relatively affluent, and they're beginning to make more and
more decisions based on their core values. They look behind the product before they buy. They reduce, reuse, and recycle. They volunteer
their time and give money to environmental and social causes in which
they believe. And they're shocked when they realize that the mutual
funds in their RRSPs hold shares of tobacco and uranium companies
and some of the most egregious polluters on the planet.

Until recently, investing in the stock and bond markets was limited
to the privileged few. But as our population has aged, with fewer workers to fund government pension plans, a growing number of people
have taken their money from under their mattresses and considered
investing it where it can actually do some good. For a generation that
boycotted Chilean grapes and South African wines, this was a natural
progression.

Social investors seek competitive returns while putting their
money to work in ways that are consistent with their personal values. A study done by the Ideation Group in Toronto revealed that
53 percent of Canadians are interested in investing in socially
screened (ethical) mutual funds. In a survey done for Calvert Mutual
Funds by Yankelovich & Partners in 1996, more than 80 percent of
people questioned about their current investments said they would
be more likely to invest in a fund if its companies did not harm the
environment.

In *Altruism, Opportunism and Points in Between: Trends and
Practices in Corporate Social Responsibility,* a report prepared for the
Insurance Corporation of British Columbia, Mark Schacter points
to a growing body of evidence that corporations are becoming more
focused on corporate social responsibility. A *Financial Times* and

PricewaterhouseCoopers survey of 750 CEOs found that they regarded pressure from stakeholders as the second-most important challenge facing them in the new millennium. Investors are also consumers, and as dual stakeholders they can change and are changing the way that companies do business. As more capital seeks clean investments, more companies will strive to meet higher standards for behaviour and accountability. This is basic supply and demand, and investors are becoming more demanding every day.

There are three key strategies that social investors can use to feel positive about their investments, influence corporate behaviour, and help build strong, sustainable communities: investment screening, shareholder action, and community investing.

Investment Screening

Interest in investment screening has increased dramatically over the past few years. The Social Investment Forum reports that in 1997 more than US$1 trillion was invested in socially and environmentally screened investments for the first time in the U.S. That number has risen to more than US$2 trillion in the past two years. One of every eight dollars in the U.S. is invested in socially or environmentally screened investments.

Investment screening involves considering a wide range of social and environmental issues. As an individual investor, you can decide which companies are suitable investments by applying investment screens based on your values.

Negative screens eliminate companies with activities or values you wish to avoid. Typical negative screens are military weapons, nuclear power, tobacco, gambling, and alcohol. Negative screening is absolutely black or white. It eliminates companies without recognizing their strengths in other areas. For instance, many social investors would screen out tobacco companies in spite of their generous contributions to the arts.

Positive or qualitative screens evaluate a company's strengths and concerns in areas such as environment, community, diversity, international operations, and human rights. Positive screening acknowledges that there are no perfect companies. This means that investors have to decide on what behaviours and practices they can accept. Unlike negative screening, positive or qualitative screening is never black or white—it is always grey. This is where investors have to make some tough choices.

Ideally, as a social investor you will seek out profitable companies with outstanding social or environmental records: Companies that support the communities in which they operate have good employer–employee relations, have excellent environmental policies and practices, make safe and useful products, and demonstrate respect for human rights at home and abroad. You can eliminate companies that produce harmful products, are major polluters, and so on. The result is an investment portfolio that meets your social criteria and produces the returns you need to achieve your financial goals.

Shareholder Action

Social investing recognizes that there are *no* perfect companies. Being a socially responsible company is not about being perfect, but about being transparent and open to dialogue with shareholders and other stakeholders. It's about being held up to public scrutiny and making changes when necessary.

As an active shareholder, you can influence corporate behaviour. You can engage in dialogue with companies by writing letters, asking questions at annual general meetings, voting your proxies or shares, and filing shareholder proposals.

Churches have been leaders in shareholder action in both Canada and the U.S. In 1975 Canadian churches established the Taskforce on the Churches and Corporate Responsibility (TCCR). TCCR was established to address issues like apartheid in South Africa and human rights abuses in Chile and other countries. In their view, companies have an obligation not only to increase profits to their shareholders but also to be good corporate citizens.

In the 1980s, TCCR focused on apartheid and successfully used shareholder action to encourage Canadian banks to reject new loans to South Africa. Without international pressure from shareholder activists, it might have taken much longer to end apartheid.

Unfortunately, the church shareholder movement peaked in the 1980s. In 1987 the Jesuits lost a controversial court ruling to Varity Corporation, an industrial management company, regarding a shareholder proposal on South African divestment. This established a precedent that has allowed companies to exclude shareholder proposals that pertain to corporate social responsibility. That ruling and a lack of significant institutional shareholder action have caused Canada to lag behind the U.S. in this area.

However, in spite of a hostile legislative environment and limited participation from institutional shareholders in Canada, there have been successes around issues like apartheid, sustainable forestry, and sweatshop and child labour. In the next year or two, shareholders likely will challenge Canada's restrictive legislation in the courts.

As well, institutional investors are finally starting to screen their investments and engage in shareholder actions. For the first time in Canada, socially screened mutual funds are using their social screening criteria as a guide when they vote on shareholder resolutions.

Community Investing

Community investing allows you to put your money directly in the hands of the people who need it most.

Technology and depleting resources have created the need for many Canadian communities to shift from resource-based economies relying on fishing and forestry to other industries. This displacement of workers has created a real need for micro-credit and seed and expansion capital for new businesses. At the same time, many banks and other institutional investors have decreased their small business investments. The need for this type of capital is enormous. Credit unions, some labour-sponsored funds, community loan funds, and social venture capitalists are trying to fill this void.

Credit unions have traditionally used their deposit money for local loans and mortgages. Some credit unions, such as B.C.'s VanCity, have lending programs that focus specifically on small business. Labour-sponsored funds have a mandate to provide equity capital to small and medium-sized businesses in order to create employment in the provinces in which they operate. For taking that risk, their unitholders are rewarded with generous tax incentives.

There are only a handful of community loan funds in Canada. They are an efficient means of providing resources for the development of new businesses. In addition to raising capital from individuals and government, there is usually a volunteer component that provides training and other resources for local enterprises.

VanCity Community Investment Deposit Loans

VanCity offers term deposits that pay 1 percent less than the market rate and uses the money to form a pool of capital that is available to finance affordable housing, job creation, and education projects. The 1 percent is offered as a rate reduction to borrowers who have been approved by an advisory committee of community experts.

Social venture capitalists are another breed altogether. Usually they are investors who are concerned as much about social and environmental issues as profitability. They seek out companies that will become strong, viable businesses, but it will take a good social story to get them interested.

Becoming a Social Investor

As you'll see in the next section, socially responsible stocks perform as well or better than stocks of companies that focus solely on financial rewards. Contrary to conventional opinion, it is possible to achieve solid financial returns by investing in companies that embrace social values similar to your own. So, how should you begin to select the most appropriate investments?

For most of you, the obvious first step is to apply social and environmental screens to your investment portfolio. In a later section, Measuring Corporate Responsibility, we discuss the most common screens that Canadians use to measure a corporation's social responsibility: community involvement, diversity in the workplace, employee relations, ethical business practices, environmental impact, human rights, and the types of products produced.

You can choose as much or as little involvement in screening companies for social responsibility as you want. Many investors choose to invest in socially screened mutual funds whose social criteria match their own. The screening criteria are outlined in the fund prospectus, and the fund administrator is responsible for screening the stocks purchased within the fund. Later we discuss some of the socially screened mutual funds currently available in Canada.

Other investors will want to take a more active role and own a screened stock and bond portfolio so that they can invest in the companies that best reflect their values. This book will help you begin to construct your own portfolio of stocks. Later we discuss the criteria we used to select the 50 stocks that appear in this book, and how you can formulate a socially responsible investment portfolio.

DOING WELL BY DOING GOOD

Your financial advisor may tell you that you can invest with a social conscience or to make money, but that you cannot do both. Adding social and environmental screens into the investment selection process, your advisor says, will only limit your choices and reduce your returns. On the contrary, you respond, companies that treat their employees well have more productive workforces than their competitors and firms with progressive environmental policies experience cost savings and avoid potential legal liabilities.

Who's right? Is socially responsible investing a choice between values and financial rewards, or can social investors have their cake and eat it, too?

The United States
It's no coincidence that most of the data highlighting the links between social responsibility and financial performance emanate from the United States, where social investing has experienced the greatest growth during the past ten years. Although we cannot review the complete array of U.S. studies here, it's important to spend some time examining a few key facts.

Mutual Funds
According to the Social Investment Forum, there are more than 70 socially responsible mutual funds available for sale in the United States. In July 1999 Morningstar, the leading provider of mutual fund research data and analysis in the U.S., published a study showing that

socially responsible mutual funds are twice as likely as all mutual funds south of the border to earn the firm's top five-star rating. Approximately 20 percent of socially responsible mutual funds earned a five-star rating through June 30, 1999, compared to just 10 percent of the total mutual fund universe. The Morningstar study stated that:

> *We see from the numbers that socially responsible mutual funds are clearly competitive with non-screened funds. And, from a risk-adjusted performance standpoint, screened funds have generally performed better than non-screened funds. This is the kind of evidence that should help put to rest the old canard that socially responsible funds are incapable of delivering competitive performance.*

Despite this glowing record, analyzing the performance of socially responsible mutual funds is not the best way to answer the question at hand. Although it provides some answers, other variables may account for the overall superior performance of socially responsible mutual funds. For example, the Morningstar study may point to the possibility that managers of socially responsible funds are more skilled than their counterparts, as much as it highlights the fact that good companies are also strong financial stocks. To deal more effectively with this issue, we must turn to a more sophisticated analysis.

Domini Social Index

The Domini Social Index (DSI) is a market capitalization–weighted, common stock index that includes 400 U.S. corporations that pass multiple, broad-based social screens. These corporations are not necessarily the 400 best social or environmental companies in the U.S., nor are they the only 400 companies that meet the social criteria highlighted in the box on the next page. Instead, the DSI reflects the general market behaviour of stocks that an average U.S. social investor might hold in his or her portfolio.

Domini Social Index Screening Criteria

The DSI does not include companies that:

- derive 2 percent or more of sales from military weapons systems,
- derive any revenue from the manufacture of alcohol or tobacco products,
- derive any revenue from providing gaming products or services,
- own interests in nuclear power plants or derive electricity from nuclear facilities, or
- on balance, have records that are negative in areas such as diversity, employee relations, the environment, and product safety.

Kinder, Lydenberg, Domini & Co., Inc., a Boston-based social investment research firm and creator of the DSI, launched the index on May 1, 1990. In the ten years since its inception, the DSI has outperformed the S&P 500, S&P MidCap, and Russell 1000 indexes. Although studies have shown that some of the DSI's strong performance is due to the specific asset selection return to the index and its smaller-cap "growth" bias, they also highlight the fact that "socially responsible investing does not necessarily preclude above-average returns." After its exhaustive study of the DSI in 1992, BARRA, a well-respected U.S. financial research firm, concluded that "...there is a specific return premium to the [DSI] over this time period which is presumably related to the social screens KLD has developed, though the 95% confidence level is not quite statistically significant."

Although the DSI provides compelling evidence that social investing offers competitive financial performance, any social investment professional will tell you that there is no guarantee with regards to future results. The DSI needs to experience an entire market cycle before any concrete conclusions can be drawn. Nonetheless, the evidence is impressive and has significantly shifted the debate within

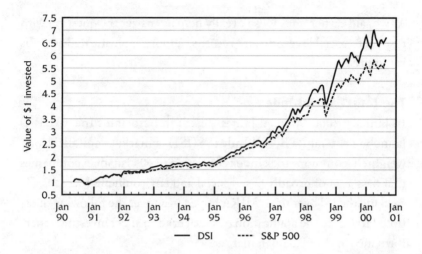

the investment community. It's no longer good enough for critics to say, "Prove to me that socially responsible investing doesn't hurt returns." It's now the critics who are challenged to prove that it does hurt returns, a job that is becoming nearly impossible given mounting evidence to the contrary.

Canada

Social investing in the U.S. market does not preclude competitive financial results. Although this is an interesting finding, it can't necessarily be transported across the border. The Canadian and U.S. financial markets are different enough that any attempt to draw conclusions from the U.S. experience would be fraught with danger. So, are social investors in Canada faced with the dilemma of investing either according to their values or to make money? Or, like their counterparts south of the border, can Canadians invest to change the world and secure their financial future at the same time?

Canadians have a variety of socially responsible mutual funds from which to choose. A review of these funds shows that some have outperformed the market while others have underperformed their peers.

As we said earlier, this doesn't really help us answer the question with respect to social investing and returns. A more sophisticated analysis is required.

The Jantzi Social Index

In January 2000 Michael Jantzi Research Associates Inc. (MJRA) launched the Jantzi Social Index™ (JSI), a market capitalization–weighted, common stock index consisting of 60 Canadian companies that pass a set of broadly based social and environmental screens. By tracking the JSI over time, MJRA hoped to answer the following question: How does the application of social criteria affect investment performance in the Canadian market?

The JSI reflects the current state of social investing in Canada, in that it is a group of stocks from which social investors might choose to invest based on a set of screening criteria (see the accompanying box). The JSI is not meant to reflect the 60 best companies in Canada, nor does it presume to represent the only 60 companies that meet social and environmental criteria.

JSI Exclusionary Screens

The JSI does not include companies that:
- are involved in the production of nuclear power,
- derive significant revenue from the manufacture of tobacco products, or
- derive significant revenue from weapons-related contracting or consulting.

The JSI seeks to avoid companies that:
- undertake questionable or fraudulent business practices,
- have a consistently poor relationship with their employees,
- demonstrate consistently poor environmental performance compared to industry counterparts,

- have experienced significant problems at their operations outside of Canada, or that operate in extremely repressive regimes, or
- manufacture unsafe products.

The JSI seeks to include companies that:
- have developed good relationships with the communities in which they operate,
- encourage diversity in the workplace,
- have strong relationships with their employees,
- have progressive environmental records, and
- have superior records of corporate governance.

Before launching the JSI, MJRA analyzed its financial performance vis-à-vis the TSE 100 and TSE 300 indexes. State Street Global Advisors (SSgA) backtested the JSI for the period of December 1994 to December 1999 and found that it outperformed all three of these benchmarks. Moreover, the JSI achieved higher returns with less risk than the TSE 100 or TSE 300. Overall, the historical results showed that the JSI was superior to the other indexes.

JSI Returns and Risk Analysis (31 December 1994–31 December 1999)

	JSI	TSE 100	TSE 300
Annualized Return	18.93%	18.11%	17.35%
Standard Deviation (Risk)	16.12%	16.04%	15.76%
Sharpe Ratio*	0.802	0.755	0.720

*(Return–Risk=Free Return)/Standard Deviation [Assumed Rf=6%]

The real test for Canadian social investors will be how the JSI performs in the future. Because the JSI has only been "live" for a short time, it is too early to draw any conclusions from the data. Nonetheless, an analysis of the JSI versus the traditional Canadian indexes shows that its performance has continued to be competitive during its first months. Although some time must pass before we can accurately determine how a group of socially responsible Canadian stocks performs versus traditional benchmarks, the initial message seems to be consistent with findings across the globe: Social investing does not hinder your financial return.

International

Social investing is growing worldwide, in part because investors can achieve competitive returns and social change in the same breath. Data highlighting the links between social responsibility and strong financial performance on the global stage correspond to findings in North America.

In September 1999 Dow Jones & Company launched its Dow Jones Sustainability Index because it believes that environmentally responsible companies have superior performance and favourable risk/return profiles. Sustainability is a catalyst for enlightened and disciplined management, a crucial success factor according to Dow Jones. The index includes more than 200 companies and represents the top 10 percent of leading sustainability companies in 73 industry groups and 33 countries. The analysis includes an examination of each company's environmental policies, programs, and performance.

The Dow Jones Sustainability Index has outperformed the traditional Dow Jones Index both in terms of historical analysis and since its launch.

Current data in Canada, the U.S., and internationally indicate that individuals can choose to invest in socially responsible companies without having to sacrifice financial return on their investments. In the following section we'll discuss the evolving nature of business ethics and the corporate social values that are most important to Canadian investors today.

MEASURING CORPORATE SOCIAL RESPONSIBILITY

If ten years ago you had asked some friends what the term *business ethics* meant, chances are they would have responded with a blank stare. There might have been a flicker of recognition before they quickly dismissed the concept as an oxymoron, like jumbo shrimp or guest host.

Traditionally, commentators described an ethical company as one that obeyed the law or implemented a business code of conduct. However, the concept of business ethics has evolved gradually into the broader and more meaningful construct of corporate social responsibility. Although some companies continue to define the term narrowly, focusing only on charitable donations, it is generally accepted that corporate social responsibility encompasses much more. That being said, there are many different definitions of corporate social responsibility, as the proliferation of corporate, national, and international codes of conduct will attest.

Fortunately, there are common themes throughout these varied definitions. For example, there seems to be some consensus that socially responsible companies pay attention to all of their stakeholders, not just shareholders. The Toronto Stock Exchange emphasizes that the "direction and management of the business should take into account the impact on other stakeholders such as employees, customers, suppliers, and communities." The Organization for Economic Cooperation and Development declares: "Corporations should recognize that the contributions of stakeholders constitute a valuable resource for building competitive and profitable companies."

So, how do we measure stakeholder interests and pick the best socially responsible companies in the stock market? It's not an easy job, because no company can boast about having an unblemished social and environmental record. The challenge is to weigh each company's performance with respect to the indicators that most social investors use to screen their portfolios. In the final analysis, the companies that make the grade will all have problems, but on balance their social performance will be superior to their counterparts that ignore the realities of the new marketplace. And according to what we learned earlier, chances are that their financial performance will follow suit.

Let's turn our attention to the screens that most social investors in Canada use to determine which companies can be considered socially responsible.

Community Involvement

Canadian companies operate in hundreds of communities across the country and in every corner of the globe. These communities are made up of the customers and employees of the firms, who interrelate on many different levels. Vibrant communities are essential to the long-term success of corporations.

Being a good corporate citizen means more than donating money to the communities in which the company operates, although that is an important measure of success. Social responsibility also means that a company consults with local communities that are affected by its operations during all aspects of decision making. This is especially true for companies that operate in regions populated predominantly by aboriginal people. A socially responsible company develops economic and community-based relationships with aboriginal communities in which the benefits of development are shared equitably.

Diversity in the Workplace

It makes good business sense for companies to tap into the largest possible talent pool they can. Those companies whose hiring and promotion practices ignore large parts of society put themselves at a competitive disadvantage vis-à-vis competitors that attract talented employees across all groups.

Being a socially responsible company means implementing programs to encourage the hiring and promotion of women, visible minorities, the disabled, or other traditionally disadvantaged groups. It means demonstrating a commitment to purchase from or contract with businesses owned by members of these groups. Socially responsible companies also have policies that help employees balance work and family responsibilities.

Employee Relations

Simply put, happy employees are productive employees, and a productive workforce means a healthier bottom line. When workers are treated with respect and have access to good benefits, they are more loyal to their employers, which leads to lower turnover rates and cost savings. A healthy workforce means less absenteeism and less downtime.

In evaluating how well companies are meeting their responsibilities to employees, it's important to measure the state of the relationship at all levels of the workforce. For example, socially responsible companies encourage worker ownership and involvement by way of employee stock ownership plans or extensive participation in management decision making throughout all levels of the organization, not only at the senior management level. They share financial successes with all workers through cash profit sharing programs. Responsible companies provide competitive benefit packages and safe workplaces.

Although union membership, in and of itself, is not an indicator of a socially responsible company, how management relates to its unionized workers is an important measure of success. Responsible companies do not undermine or interfere with the employees' right to organize. And although socially responsible companies may be forced to downsize their operations from time to time, they provide displaced employees with assistance, including retraining or other job opportunities.

Environment

Companies that implement progressive environmental policies and introduce leading-edge technologies are more likely to avoid costly legal liabilities and often experience production cost savings. In addition, environmental performance is one of the key indicators of corporate social responsibility for Canadians, according to numerous polls and market research studies.

Environics Poll (http://www.environics.net/eil/millennium/)

In 1999 Environics developed the Millennium Poll on Corporate Social Responsibility, which surveyed representative samples of 1000 citizens in each of 23 countries on 6 continents. According to Environics' president, "The findings from the Millennium Poll underline the importance of major companies having an active corporate function to address how they can help contribute to the social and environmental, as well as the economic agenda of the countries in which they operate."

Like citizens worldwide, Canadians say that the role of business is to make profits and create jobs, but far more important over the next decade will be helping build a better society. In fact, Canadians are among the most adamant about companies adopting a broader role. Only 11 percent of Canadians think that companies should focus solely on making a profit, paying taxes, employing people, and obeying laws. Four times as many (43 percent) think that companies should work to exceed lawful requirements, set higher ethical standards, and help build a better society for all. The remainder thinks that companies should operate somewhere between these extremes.

Worldwide, 33 percent say that they form impressions of a company based on business fundamentals such as financial factors, company size, business strategy, or management; 40 percent mention brand quality or corporate image or reputation. A majority (almost 60 percent) mentions factors related to companies' broader responsibilities: labour practices, business ethics, responsibility to society at large, or environmental impact.

Socially responsible companies implement outstanding environmental management and reporting systems and engage in exceptional environmental planning, impact assessment, and meaningful public consultation as part of their decision-making process. They are committed to efficient and environmentally sound use of natural resources through extensive use of recycled materials and alternative energy sources. They not only comply with applicable laws and regulations, but also strive to reduce the environmental impact of their operations, resulting in major reductions in the use and release of toxins, hazardous substances, and other pollutants. Socially responsible companies also develop products or services that have environmental benefits.

Best of Sector

In evaluating a company's overall environmental performance record, Michael Jantzi Research Associates Inc. uses the Best-of-Sector™ (BoS) methodology. Companies are not expected to demonstrate "perfect" behaviour, as each firm is measured against the best practices in its industry. By evaluating companies in relation to their industry counterparts, social investors can avoid disqualifying entire sectors for investment. The BoS approach is also consistent with the underlying goal of encouraging positive corporate change, a central goal of the social investment movement. It provides an incentive for companies in sectors that face environmental challenges to improve their performance. Therefore, the BoS investment screening methodology is both financially prudent and consistent with the underlying goals of most social investors in Canada.

Human Rights

Globalization has taken hold and companies are now players on the world stage. Therefore, when measuring a firm's commitment to corporate social responsibility it's important to evaluate its operations internationally, not just those in our own backyard. Socially responsible companies respect communities and indigenous peoples and have implemented progressive labour and environmental standards at their overseas operations. They have also implemented or participate in credible and independently monitored mechanisms to ensure that their suppliers and subcontractors do not contribute to human rights abuses, unfair or abusive labour practices, or environmental degradation.

When companies operate overseas, especially in less developed economies, they often face human rights challenges. How can we most effectively measure whether a company is acting responsibly with respect to human rights issues?

Some social investment professionals argue that socially responsible companies avoid operating in countries in which human rights abuses are widespread. Michael Jantzi Research Associates Inc.'s approach to corporate social responsibility on the international and human rights front is somewhat different. It evaluates a company's social performance in the international arena on a case-by-case basis, examining the specific impact of the corporation rather than the location of its operations. Implicit in this "company-specific" approach, as opposed to a "country-specific" approach, is the belief that investment in less developed economies can have a positive *or* negative impact on the citizens of the host country. Investment can provide jobs and raise the standard of living in these countries, or it can cause significant social and environmental damage. Socially responsible companies support the former and avoid the latter.

However, there are some countries in which it is impossible for companies to operate without supporting governments that seriously abuse human rights and in which no level of corporate engagement can have a positive impact. For example, socially responsible companies avoid operating in countries such as Burma and Sudan. The human rights abuses perpetrated by the ruling regime in Burma are among the most severe in the world, and many human rights organizations are urging economic sanctions against the country. In Sudan the oil companies fuel the government coffers, allowing it to wage war against its own citizens.

Product and Practices

Socially responsible companies ensure that they obey applicable laws and industry standards with respect to advertising, marketing, and production practices. They do not engage in price fixing, antitrust activities, consumer frauds, or other illegal business initiatives. Also, it's a simple concept, but one that bears repeating: Socially responsible companies manufacture safe products. This is not only an important pillar of corporate social responsibility, but also makes good business sense.

In addition, a company's commitment to social responsibility is measured in some circles according to the types of products it produces. For example, some would argue that socially responsible companies are not involved in the production of military weapons, nuclear power, or tobacco products.

Military Weapons

Although national defence is necessary to maintain sovereignty, arms proliferation breeds violence and creates an increased demand for weapons. In many societies, military expenditures limit social and economic options; resources would be better focused on health, education, and human development. Accordingly, manufacturers of weapons do not fit the definition of socially responsible companies for many social investors.

Nuclear Energy

Some social investors argue that no matter how progressive their policies might be in other areas, companies involved in the nuclear energy industry cannot be defined as socially responsible. There is widespread concern about the environmental impact of uranium mining and its impact on the health of workers. With respect to power generation, the long-term effects associated with the storage of nuclear waste are uncertain. There are also issues related to the interrelationship of uranium mining, power generation, and the production of nuclear weapons. Above all, there are concerns about the risk of nuclear accidents exposing workers and local communities to lethal doses of radiation. Accordingly, in the opinion of many Canadians, socially responsible companies develop non-nuclear, renewable, and cleaner energy alternatives such as co-generation, fuel cell, solar, wind, and geothermal technologies.

Tobacco

Most social investors view tobacco companies as the antithesis of social responsibility. Tobacco is the only legal substance that harms human health even at moderate levels of use. It has been clinically proven that smoking is linked to cancer and other diseases. In fact, smoking is the most significant cause of preventable illness, disability, and premature death in Canada. Moreover, there is evidence that tobacco companies have targeted their marketing initiatives at the most vulnerable elements of society, primarily children. The federal government has also named tobacco companies in lawsuits for smuggling cigarettes across international borders in eastern Canada.

Now that we have defined social investing, discussed its viability in terms of return on investment, and examined the social screens that most Canadians consider to be important, it's time to explain how we chose the 50 stocks that appear in this book and how you can begin to select and build your own portfolio of socially responsible stocks or mutual funds.

MUTUAL FUNDS OR A STOCK PORTFOLIO?

The Basics

To achieve your financial goals, you should develop a sound financial plan that incorporates your investment objectives, time horizon, and risk tolerance. Finding a trusted financial advisor or planner is an important part of this process.

The types of investments you choose may determine whether you reach your goal. Portfolio diversification is important because it reduces volatility and, therefore, reduces risk. You should diversify among several asset classes such as common stocks, bonds, and short-term guaranteed investments such as Treasury bills (T-bills) and guaranteed investment certificates (GICs). Historically, over the past 50 years, common stocks (and by association, equity mutual funds) have almost doubled the return of bonds and T-bills. However, to achieve that level of growth, you have to be prepared for market volatility.

The decision whether to invest in mutual funds or stocks for the equity portion of your portfolio usually depends on your financial goals. Your investment objectives, risk tolerance, and time horizon must be considered when you make this decision. For some of you, the best decision may be not to invest in either vehicle.

If you're going to become anxious every time your portfolio drops in value, stick to guaranteed investments like T-bills or GICs. You'll sleep better at night, but don't fool yourself into thinking that these are risk-free investments simply because you get your money back when they mature. If inflation rears its ugly head, you could actually lose money on those investments if you have to pay tax on the income (i.e., if annual inflation increases to 5 percent and your GIC is only paying 4 percent or even less).

If you're just starting your investment portfolio or you're contributing to a monthly savings and investment plan, diversification is most easily accomplished by investing in socially screened mutual funds. In Canada, more than 200,000 mutual fund investors have made investment decisions that integrate their financial needs and social values.

Socially Screened Mutual Funds

The Pioneer Fund was founded in the United States in 1928 for investors who wanted to avoid investing in tobacco and alcohol stocks. Today, America's largest family of socially screened funds, The Calvert Group, has socially screened assets of over US$2.5 billion. The growth in screened assets has been staggering. Socially screened mutual funds in the U.S. have over $154 billion in assets.

The Social Investment Organization (SIO) reports that, in 1987, there were just a handful of socially screened mutual funds in Canada, with about $10 million in assets. By 1997 there were 14 socially screened funds with total assets of just under $2 billion. Screened assets increased 200 times in that time period compared to less than 15 times for unscreened assets.

As of September 2000 there were 24 socially and environmentally screened mutual funds to choose from in Canada, although this number is expected to increase with some new offerings early in 2001. Like all mutual funds, a socially screened fund is a pool of money invested in stocks, bonds, or other securities. These funds differ in that each fund screens its investments according to social and environmental criteria and publishes those criteria in its prospectus.

Certain funds focus on specific areas such as sustainable development, while others invest in companies that are the best in their sector. As an investor, you will need to research individual funds to find the ones best suited to your own values.

The first socially screened mutual fund in Canada was the Ethical Growth Fund, launched by Vancouver City Savings Credit Union in 1986. Since then, this fund family has grown to 12 funds and about $2 billion in assets. Mutual fund guru Gordon Pape named Ethical Growth "Fund of the Year" in his *1998 Buyer's Guide to Mutual Funds*.

The Ethical family of funds are screened with the best-of-sector approach on the basis of industrial relations, racial equality, tobacco, military, nuclear energy, and environmental practices. Ethical Funds also encourage companies to respect the environment and basic human rights. It is the only screened mutual fund company in Canada to engage in dialogue with corporations over issues raised by its screening and proxy voting guidelines.

The Clean Environment family has three funds managed by Acuity Funds Inc. Its objective is to "seek out exceptional companies poised for significant growth and which provide goods and services consistent with the principles of sustainable development." Fund manager Ian Ihnatowycz describes sustainable development as "economic growth with technologies that do not destroy our planet."

Desjardins Funds in Quebec offers the Desjardins Environment Fund. The objective of this fund is to invest in Quebec and Canadian companies whose activities contribute significantly to maintaining or improving the environment. The fund manager must choose securities that meet the fund's environmental criteria. Desjardins Funds also has three other screened funds that hold units of various funds from the Ethical group.

Mackenzie recently launched the Universal Global Ethics Fund. Although it is relatively new, its American and British managers have many years of experience in managing successful socially screened funds in those countries. It invests in companies in any country that are socially responsible in conducting their business operations.

The Navigator SAMI Fund invests in companies that fit screening criteria developed to be consistent with the precepts of Koranic law. Companies inconsistent with this fund include those whose primary businesses are in the areas of alcohol, tobacco, pork- and poultry-related products, financial services (usury and interest-generating business activities), defence and weapons, and entertainment.

The SUMMA fund is an Investors Group mutual fund and boasts the best return of all of that institution's Canadian equity funds over all time periods. The $3 billion fund screens out companies involved in alcohol, gambling, weapons, pornography, and tobacco. It also screens out companies that do not have effective environmental policies and those that support repressive regimes.

YMG Funds established the YMG Sustainable Development Fund in May 1999. The objective of the fund is to provide long-term capital growth and safety of principal through investment in blue-chip companies with a quantifiable commitment to sustainable development.

For many social investors, mutual funds do not provide the level of screening they need to feel comfortable with their investments. The alternative is to buy stocks that have been screened according to their own values. This book is aimed at helping those investors.

The Best 50 Stocks

If you can withstand the volatility and you have enough savings to diversify your portfolio, you may want to consider investing the equity component of your portfolio in individual stocks.

In this book we've put together a portfolio of 50 stocks that have been screened according to broad-based social and environmental criteria, in addition to financial criteria.

Some of these companies may be suitable for your portfolio. Of course, you should discuss any investment choices with your financial advisor to ensure that they fit your overall investment objectives.

Choosing the Companies

While choosing the stocks for this book we encountered a number of challenges. Since we had to balance financial and social criteria, a number of small companies with interesting social or environmental stories didn't make the grade. Unfortunately, they didn't pass our financial criteria.

We also had to compromise in the technology sector, since it represents a significant component of the Canadian economy. There simply aren't many stellar companies on the social side, so we have included some companies that are neutral rather than exceptional. This was a big disappointment and we hope that future editions will show improvement in this sector as these companies grow and develop policies in areas such as community, diversity, employee relations, and environment.

We have included as many sectors as possible in this book. We recognize the implications of our consumption needs as Canadians. For example, many of us drive cars and consume products that require fossil fuels and a variety of minerals. We chose companies that were best in their sectors and gave preference to those with a focus on alternative technologies and best practices in their industry.

Social Screening Criteria

In choosing the stocks for this book, we screened out companies that:

- derive significant revenue from weapons-related contracting,
- derive significant revenue from the manufacture of tobacco products,
- derive significant revenue from gambling, or
- produce nuclear power.

We used social research provided by Michael Jantzi Research Associates Inc. (**www.mjra-jsi.com**) and its partners in Sustainable

Investment Research International Group (**www.sirigroup.org**), primarily Boston-based Kinder, Lydenberg, Domini & Co., Inc. (**www.kld.com**), and CaringCompany AB in Sweden, to evaluate companies' records in areas such as community (including aboriginal communities), diversity, employee relations, the environment, international operations and human rights, and product quality and business practices. We excluded companies whose records are consistently poor in those areas and looked for companies that fit one or more of the following criteria:

• are leaders in their sector in terms of best practice
• provide an environmentally or socially superior product or service
• have a strong social story (multiple strengths)

Problems in one area did not disqualify a company automatically. We recognize that no company is perfect and have tried to balance the strengths and concerns the companies have in each area. A ratings chart ranks each company in terms of community, diversity, employee relations, environment, international operations/human rights, and products and practices. Each star represents one ratings point. A company that is neutral (that is, one that has no significant strengths or concerns in an area) received three points. If there was a concern in an area, one point was deducted and the company only received two points. Additional concerns led to more points being deducted. We have not included companies that rated less than two points in any area. If a company had strengths in an area, it received additional points to a maximum of five. For example, Bank of Nova Scotia is neutral on environment and product and practices (three points each), strong on community, employee relations, and international operations (four points each), and very strong on diversity (five points). Its ratings chart looks like this:

Bank of Nova Scotia

Community	★ ★ ★ ★
Diversity	★ ★ ★ ★ ★
Employee	★ ★ ★ ★
Environment	★ ★ ★
International Operations/ Human Rights	★ ★ ★ ★
Product and Practices	★ ★ ★

Financial Screening Criteria

In selecting the stocks for this book, we considered factors such as quality of management, earnings momentum, insider trading, share repurchase, market liquidity, price/earnings, price/sales, technical indicators, analyst consensus, and sector support.

We looked at different sets of financial screening criteria depending on the size of the companies. With the larger, blue-chip companies we looked for sector leadership with consistent earnings growth at a reasonable price when possible. With smaller companies we focused on leading-edge sectors with innovative products and services and healthy balance sheets. Quality of management was an important factor in each company profile.

We've diversified the portfolio on the basis of company size and among a number of different countries and sectors. Because many Canadians invest inside RRSPs, we have selected 30 Canadian companies. And because international markets have historically outperformed the TSE 300 by almost 3 percent per year over the past 50 years, we've included 20 U.S. and a number of European companies.

How to Invest in the 50 Best Stocks

Once you have read about the 50 socially responsible stocks included in this book, you can begin to build your own portfolio:

1. Consult a financial advisor and develop a long-term financial plan that integrates your values, investment objectives, risk tolerance, and time horizon. Many of the companies we've selected are smaller capitalization companies that are not suitable for all investors.
2. Select the companies that best reflect your personal values and financial needs.
3. Consult your financial advisor to ensure that the companies you've chosen are suitable for your investment objectives.
4. Be an investor, not a speculator. Investors buy stocks of good companies and hold them for the long term.

1

AMERICAN EXPRESS CO.

World Financial Center
200 Vesey Street
New York, NY 10285
(212) 640-2000
www.americanexpress.com
AXP (NYSE)

Chairman and CEO: Harvey Golub
President and COO: Kenneth I. Chenault

Community	★ ★ ★
Diversity	★ ★ ★ ★ ★
Employee	★ ★ ★ ★
Environment	★ ★ ★
International Operations/ Human Rights	★ ★ ★
Product and Practices	★ ★ ★

American Express is a diversified financial services company best
known for its American Express Card and American Express Traveler's
Cheques. It is also a leader in travel services. American Express is expanding its strong brand internationally, increasing its product offerings, and building its credit card network. It has been introducing
new co-branded credit cards and membership rewards targeted at

specific markets. The Financial Advisors unit continues to show strong growth from sales of mutual funds and other products and is benefiting from higher-than-average fees on assets under administration. Like many credit card companies, American Express has positioned itself to benefit from Internet opportunities.

American Express has a paid sabbatical program that allows long-service employees to work in community service or education. The company created the Volunteer Action Fund in 1994, which awards grants on a competitive basis to eligible organizations at which employees regularly volunteer their time.

In 1991 American Express established a senior executive diversity council. The company has employee diversity teams and provides diversity training to employees and managers. It also links management compensation to an employee's ability to meet diversity goals, integrate diversity considerations into business functions, and address diversity concerns raised in annual employee surveys. One minority member serves among the ranks of American Express' five senior executives. Two women and two minority members serve on the company's 15-member board of directors. This level of diversity at senior management and board levels is rare in corporate America.

American Express' policies promote flextime, telecommuting, compressed workweeks, and job sharing at all company locations. Manager pay is tied to both employee satisfaction and the use of flextime. Child-care benefits include free backup care, before- and after-school care, pre-tax set-asides, and resource and referral services for both child care and elder care.

For substantially all of its domestic employees, American Express has a defined benefit pension plan. In 1995 the company amended the plan so that a retiring employee may take a lump-sum payment instead of monthly payments. In addition, American Express' retirement options include a 401(k) savings plan through which the company matches, in company stock, 100 percent of employees' contributions up to 3 percent of base compensation.

American Express Financial Advisors' Minneapolis office offers employees subsidized, all-you-can-ride bus passes to encourage bus use. The company began a program of environmental audits at its U.S. facilities in 1994.

American Express initiated a formal total quality management program in 1991 based on the criteria for the Malcolm Baldrige National Quality Award. The company has developed systems to analyze its performance relating to customers, employees, and shareholders. As part of the quality program, American Express uses formal benchmarking guidelines. Since 1990 the Chairman's Award for Quality has recognized quality teams, both for their results and for how they achieve them. The company annually surveys employees about how well management is performing in achieving stated objectives and values.

The company's CEO received a compensation package valued at US$10.9 million in fiscal 1998, including a non-cash component consisting primarily of stock options valued at approximately US$3.8 million.

In February 1999 a French government–appointed panel reported that five U.S. companies with banking operations in France during the Second World War, including American Express, had handed over accounts of Jewish customers to Nazi occupiers. A spokesperson for American Express stated that the company had been reviewing archives and "was not aware of any American Express accounts turned over to the authorities."

American Express Co. at a Glance

Fiscal year ended: December 31

Revenue in US$ millions

	1995	1996	1997	1998	1999
Total Revenue ($)	15,841	15,900	17,760	19,132	21,278
Earnings/ Share ($)	1.02	1.3	1.38	1.54	1.81
Price to Earnings (PE)	13.3	15.87	21.45	22.14	30.67
Dividend Yield (%)	2.18	1.59	1.01	0.88	0.54

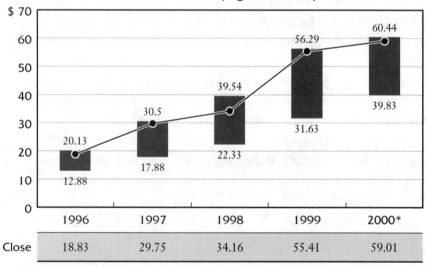

Stock Growth (High-Low-Close)

	1996	1997	1998	1999	2000*
Close	18.83	29.75	34.16	55.41	59.01

*2000 price as of August 31

2
ASTROPOWER INC.

Solar Park
Newark, DE 19716-2000
(302) 366-0400
www.astropower.com
APWR (NASDAQ)

President and CEO: Dr. Allen M. Barnett

Community	★ ★ ★
Diversity	★ ★ ★
Employee	★ ★ ★ ★
Environment	★ ★ ★ ★
International Operations/ Human Rights	★ ★ ★
Product and Practices	★ ★ ★

AstroPower develops, manufactures, and markets photovoltaic solar cells, modules, and panels for generating solar electric power. Existing electric utility customers who want clean, renewable electric power use solar power in on-grid applications. Solar power is also used off-grid in a variety of applications in rural areas. The company also manufactures and markets single-crystal silicon solar cells and modules worldwide and is developing specialty photovoltaic devices and detectors. In May 2000 AstroPower introduced a new line of eight-inch solar cells and power modules. The company has been a leader in the shift to larger, more cost-effective solar cell configurations. AstroPower is one of the fastest growing solar electric power companies. Its growth is driven by increasing demand for "green power" generation programs due to deregulation and customer choice.

AstroPower gives at least 100 stock options to every employee at time of hiring. As well, the company grants additional options to each employee after every five years of employment. AstroPower also gives cash bonuses to employees when it achieves certain financial goals. For almost all of its employees, AstroPower has 401(k) savings plan through which it matches a portion of employee contributions up to a percentage of base compensation.

AstroPower has a formal environmental policy, as well as a formal environment management system. The company conducts regular environmental audits of its operations, either monthly or quarterly, depending on the manufacturing process involved. AstroPower has a full-time environmental engineer. This person reports to the manager of manufacturing engineering, who is responsible for the firm's environmental systems.

Among AstroPower's environmentally progressive manufacturing practices is the use of silicon wafers. AstroPower recycles these wafers, discarded by the computer chip industry, for use in its products. The company reports that it has an informal energy efficiency program.

AstroPower is on the leading edge in terms of developing the crucial element in solar energy production, the photovoltaic cell. In late 1998 the company received two research contracts from the U.S. Department of Energy. The first was for additional research on photovoltaic manufacturing technologies. The second was for additional research on the assembly of solar energy modules from solar cells.

In 1997 AstroPower entered into a joint venture called GPU Solar with GPU International, a subsidiary of GPU, Inc. in the United States. GPU Solar plans to market rooftop solar panels in the U.S.

In addition to its research on solar cells, AstroPower reports that it is engaged in research and development on optoelectronic products—devices that convert light into electrical signals. This research has been funded by, among others, the U.S. Air Force, the Ballistic Missile Defense Organization, and the Defense Advanced Research Projects Agency. In the U.S., much advanced technology is funded by the Department of Defense (DoD). Because solar energy has applications in space flight, the U.S. federal government, both through NASA and the DoD, historically has supported considerable research in this area.

AstroPower reports that it derives less than 1 percent of its annual revenue, including research grants and contracts, from the DoD. Most of its products have both civilian and military applications, and none of them are weapons-related.

AstroPower Inc. at a Glance

Fiscal year ended: December 31

Revenue in US$ millions

	1995	1996	1997	1998	1999
Total Revenue ($)	9	10	16	23	34
Earnings/ Share ($)	–	–	0.13	0.28	0.22
Price to Earnings (PE)	–	–	–	56.62	60.87
Dividend Yield (%)	–	–	–	–	–

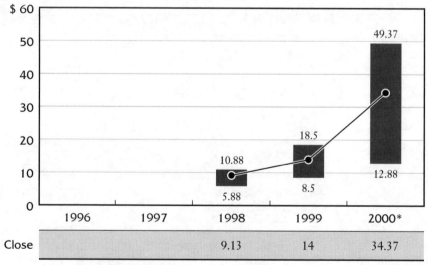

Stock Growth (High-Low-Close)

	1998	1999	2000*
Close	9.13	14	34.37

*2000 price as of August 31

3

BALLARD POWER SYSTEMS INC.

9000 Glenlyon Parkway
Burnaby, BC V5J 5J9
(604) 454-0900
www.ballard.com
BLD (TSE, NASDAQ)

Chairman and CEO: Firoz A. Rasul
President: Layle K. Smith

Community	★ ★ ★
Diversity	★ ★ ★
Employee	★ ★ ★ ★
Environment	★ ★ ★ ★
International Operations/ Human Rights	★ ★ ★
Product and Practices	★ ★ ★

Ballard Power Systems develops proton exchange membrane (PEM) fuel cells for zero-emission engines used in automobiles, stationary power plants, transit buses, and marine and surface vessels.

Ballard Power Systems' PEM fuel cell converts energy from a fuel source into electricity without combustion. The fuel cells are being developed to use hydrogen, and therefore operate with significantly reduced emissions of air pollutants such as carbon dioxide, nitrogen oxides, particulates, or unburned hydrocarbons, which normally are associated with conventional internal combustion engines. The hydrogen fuel cell's only by-product is water vapour. Nevertheless, some of the fuels used in Ballard Power Systems' cells are refined from petrochemicals, a non-renewable resource whose refining leads to emissions that cause global warming and acid rain.

Not for the timid investor, this stock is extremely volatile and has always been driven by news. Look for ongoing reports about increased product prototypes, stationary power plant contracts, legislative changes, and new partnerships to keep up in this sector. The company is making progress on reducing costs to compete with traditional technologies. Although hybrid vehicles are charging all over the place, California regulators are adamant about seeing zero-emission technology in the near future.

As fuel cell companies have received increasing attention, the market has begun to differentiate them by considering their strategic partnerships. Ballard's clients and partners include DaimlerChrysler, Ford, Honda, General Motors, and Nissan. DaimlerChrysler and Ford introduced new fuel cell–powered vehicles in late 1998 and the first quarter of 1999, respectively. During the past three years, Ballard has secured automotive contracts from Volkswagen AG and AB Volvo.

Ballard Power Systems is implementing an employment equity program. Although none of its ten board directors or seven senior officers is female, the company offers employees flextime and job sharing to help them balance work and family responsibilities.

All directors, officers, employees, and consultants of Ballard Power Systems and its subsidiaries are eligible to participate in the company's share option plan. Ballard Power also awards shares to employees of the company and its subsidiaries on a discretionary basis through its share distribution plan.

Ballard Power Systems has implemented a closed-loop cooling system for its testing operations, which eliminates most of the operation's waste water. The company's development activities include an assessment and incorporation of "end of life" reuse/recycling strategies in its product design.

Ballard Power Systems' first opportunity to develop a PEM fuel cell arose from a contract with the Canadian Department of National Defence (DND) in 1983. Other military contracts have included a relationship with Howaldswerke-Deutsche Werft AG (HDW) to develop fuel cell power plants for marine vessels, including submarines. HDW builds submarines for the German navy and for export. In October 1998 Ballard Power Systems teamed up with U.S.-based McDermott Technology, Inc. to secure a contract with the U.S. Navy to develop a Ship Service Fuel Cell generator.

In fiscal 1998 Ballard Power Systems' revenue from military contracts was $1.7 million, or 7 percent of total revenue. This was an increase from the $1.1 million in military contract revenue received in fiscal 1997, which represented 2 percent of total revenue. Although its revenue from military contracts is above the 5 percent we usually consider to be acceptable, Ballard Power is still very much an R&D story and it reports that defence contracts are not considered a growth area as its products enter the commercial market.

Ballard Power Systems Inc. at a Glance

Fiscal year ended: December 31

Revenue in CDN$ millions

	1995	1996	1997	1998	1999
Total Revenue ($)	21	25	24	25	33
Earnings/ Share ($)	-0.71	-0.43	0.11	0.01	-0.89
Price to Earnings (PE)	N/A	N/A	N/A	N/A	N/A
Dividend Yield (%)	N/A	N/A	N/A	N/A	N/A

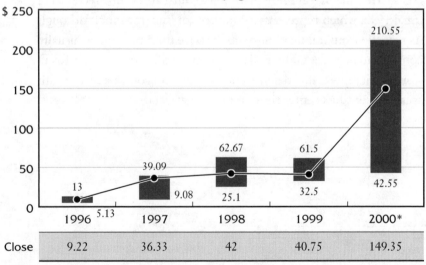

Stock Growth (High-Low-Close)

Close	9.22	36.33	42	40.75	149.35

*2000 price as of August 31

4

BANK OF MONTREAL

21st Floor, 100 King Street West
Toronto, ON M5X 1A1
(416) 867-6785
www.bmo.com
BMO (TSE)

Chairman and CEO: F. Anthony Comper
President: L. Jacques Menard

Community	★ ★ ★ ★
Diversity	★ ★ ★ ★ ★
Employee	★ ★ ★
Environment	★ ★ ★
International Operations/ Human Rights	★ ★ ★
Product and Practices	★ ★ ★ ★

The Bank of Montreal is Canada's oldest bank. It has approximately $230 billion in assets with 1198 branches in Canada and 151 offices around the world. Harris Bank, a wholly owned bank subsidiary, is based in Chicago and serves close to 1 million U.S. customers. It typically contributes more than 25 percent of Bank of Montreal's total retail bank and wealth management earnings. Bank of Montreal has a strong reputation for Internet initiatives. In 1999 the bank rolled out the first mobile banking initiative in Canada, which uses Bell's Mobility Browser capability to provide customers with user-friendly access to brokerage services.

With strong earnings growth and price performance, Canadian banks have been among the best performing bank sectors worldwide in the past year. And finally, since Financial Services Bill C-38 was introduced, the regulatory environment for bank mergers is clearly friendlier to bank customers than it was a few years ago.

Between fiscal 1996 and 1998, Bank of Montreal and its subsidiaries donated $52 million to charity, representing approximately 1 percent of pre-tax profits. Through its Volunteer Grants Program, the bank provides $500,000 annually to charitable and community groups for which employees and pensioners volunteer. Bank of Montreal employees may take both short-term and long-term leaves to participate in voluntary activities.

Bank of Montreal has a formal workplace equality policy, an Office of Workplace Equality, and a President's Advisory Council on the Equitable Workplace. It ranks first out of eight companies in the banking sector with respect to employing women in the senior officer ranks (21.9 percent). Three of its 17 board directors are women, a level of representation that is rare in corporate Canada.

Bank of Montreal offers a wide range of benefits, including a variety of flexible work arrangements. The bank subscribes to a child-care referral service, and employs one full-time and two part-time gerontologists to provide elder-care services. The bank has formed partnerships with school boards, businesses, and community organizations to provide training, mentoring, and development for visible minority youth in an effort to improve their self-esteem, leadership, and technology-related skills. Bank of Montreal also works to identify and remove barriers that prevent employees with disabilities from contributing fully.

Bank of Montreal applies its environmental policy to all internal operations, and to its relationships with customers and suppliers. The bank makes "reasonable efforts" to ensure that it provides loans only to borrowers that maintain responsible environmental management programs and comply with applicable environmental laws and regulations.

Bank of Montreal has 18 branches in aboriginal communities across Canada. It has developed a special financing program to allow residents of native reserves to be eligible for mortgages. This program circumvents restrictions in the federal Indian Act that prohibit reserve residents from owning property.

Bank of Montreal has a 16 percent interest in Grupo Financiero Bancomer SA, Mexico's second-largest financial services group. In March 1999 U.S. authorities found Bancomer guilty of laundering money in the U.S. for Mexican and Colombian drug gangs. The bank paid US$500,000 in fines and forfeited US$9.4 million seized by U.S. authorities.

Some anti-poverty and social justice organizations assert that low-income Canadians face systemic barriers to basic banking services, including unnecessarily stringent personal identification requirements for opening an account and mandatory holds placed on cheques. While the major Canadian banks have adopted new voluntary rules regarding requirements for opening and using personal bank accounts, critics claim that these voluntary measures are ineffective.

Bank of Montreal at a Glance

Fiscal year ended: October 31

Revenue in CDN$ millions

	1995	1996	1997	1998	1999
Total Revenue ($)	12,086	13,000	14,515	17,239	16,685
Earnings/ Share ($)	3.38	4.13	4.62	4.66	4.75
Price to Earnings (PE)	8.99	10.36	13.51	13.18	10.36
Dividend Yield (%)	4.26	3.39	2.59	2.85	3.81

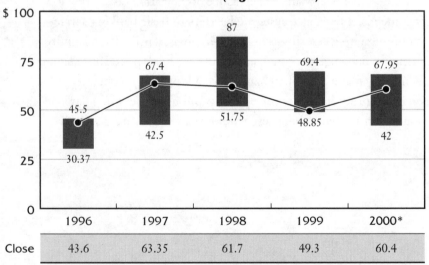

Stock Growth (High-Low-Close)

	1996	1997	1998	1999	2000*
Close	43.6	63.35	61.7	49.3	60.4

*2000 price as of August 31

5

THE BANK OF NOVA SCOTIA

44 King Street West
Toronto, ON M5H 1H1
(416) 866-3925
www.scotiabank.com
BNS (TSE)

Chairman and CEO: Peter C. Godsoe
President: Bruce R. Birmingham

Community	★ ★ ★ ★
Diversity	★ ★ ★ ★ ★
Employee	★ ★ ★ ★
Environment	★ ★ ★
International Operations/ Human Rights	★ ★ ★ ★
Product and Practices	★ ★ ★

The Bank of Nova Scotia (Scotiabank) is Canada's third-largest bank in terms of assets ($244 billion as of June 2000) and market capitalization. It operates corporate banking, retail, commercial, and trust services in more than 50 countries worldwide. It has more exposure to international markets than other Canadian banks, which is reflected in its charitable giving and international micro-lending programs. Scotiabank derives about 50 percent of its earnings outside of Canada and has benefited from strong growth in international markets.

The increasing financial needs of Canada's maturing population have and will continue to drive domestic earnings. Like all of the "Big Five" Canadian banks, Scotiabank pays an attractive dividend that increases regularly and trades at a price-to-earnings ratio that is significantly lower than that of the average stock in the TSE 300. International diversification, in terms of both financial and social criteria, makes Scotiabank one of the most attractive Canadian banks. Like the other banks, Scotiabank has experienced strong earnings growth and price performance.

Between 1996 and 1998 Scotiabank donated about $43 million to charity, representing 1 percent of the bank's pre-tax profits in each of those years. Scotiabank is a long-time supporter of the Canadian Organization for Development through Education, which provides books and educational materials to students in developing countries.

Scotiabank has formal employment equity and human rights policies. It ranks third out of eight companies in its industry sector with respect to employing women in senior officer ranks (12.5 percent). Four of the bank's 26 board directors are women, a level of representation that is rare in corporate Canada. Scotiabank's alternative work arrangement program, which helps employees balance work and family life, provides for flextime, job sharing, compressed workweeks, and telecommuting. The bank also has an employee share ownership and incentive pay program.

Scotiabank has a written policy on the environment. In January 1993 the bank established an environmental policy department to expand and pursue environmental initiatives. Scotiabank has formally endorsed the Statement by Banks on the Environment and Sustainable Development under the auspices of the United Nations. Scotiabank recycles 90 percent of its toner cartridges and paper, much of which is acid-free. The bank's print shop uses soy-based inks. Environmental considerations are included in the bank's procurement decisions.

One factor that distinguishes Scotiabank from its counterparts is that its international banking division operates Scotia Enterprise, a micro-lending program. Based in Georgetown, Guyana, the program follows the Grameen Bank model of community lending. Scotiabank reports that over 3000 loans have been dispersed, mostly to women.

Some anti-poverty and social justice organizations assert that low-income Canadians face systemic barriers to basic banking services, including unnecessarily stringent personal identification requirements for opening an account and mandatory holds placed on cheques. In 1997 the Canadian Bankers Association (CBA) released voluntary rules regarding requirements for opening and using personal bank accounts. Although the CBA reports that all major banks in Canada are adopting the new rules, some groups such as National Council of Welfare and the Canadian Community Reinvestment Coalition (CCRC) claim that the voluntary measures are ineffective. The CCRC also argues that banks should be forced to disclose more detailed information about their lending policies, as their U.S. counterparts must do under the *U.S. Community Reinvestment Act*.

The Bank of Nova Scotia at a Glance

Fiscal year ended: October 31

Revenue in CDN$ millions

	1995	1996	1997	1998	1999
Total Revenue ($)	12,093	12,402	13,171	15,949	16,654
Earnings/ Share ($)	1.69	2.04	2.95	2.64	2.93
Price to Earnings (PE)	8.84	11.24	11.4	12.78	10.6
Dividend Yield (%)	4.15	2.84	2.2	2.37	2.9

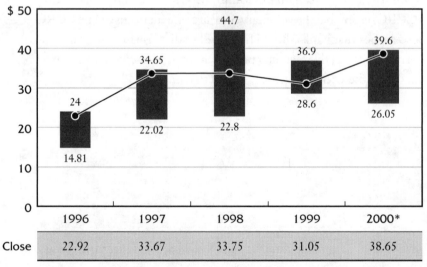

Stock Growth (High-Low-Close)

	1996	1997	1998	1999	2000*
Close	22.92	33.67	33.75	31.05	38.65

*2000 price as of August 31

6

BCE INC.

Bureau 3700, 1000 Rue de la Gauchetière Ouest
Montreal, PQ H3B 4Y7
(514) 397-7000
www.bce.ca
BCE (TSE)

Chairman, President, and CEO: Jean Monty

Community	★ ★ ★
Diversity	★ ★ ★ ★
Employee	★ ★
Environment	★ ★ ★
International Operations/ Human Rights	★ ★ ★
Product and Practices	★ ★ ★

BCE is Canada's largest telecommunications company, providing telecom services to approximately 70 percent of the Canadian population. BCE owns several very attractive telecom and e-commerce franchises, including BCE Emergis, CGI Group, Bell Nexxia, Bell Canada International, and Teleglobe. These growth stories plus 80-percent-owned Bell Canada, Canada's largest integrated telecom services provider, result in a stock with compelling value. BCE also purchased CTV in February 2000, a deal that gives BCE proprietary content.

With lots of cash, BCE is well positioned to pursue growth opportunities both domestically and internationally. In May 2000, BCE spun off most of its nearly 40 percent controlling stake in Nortel Networks to its shareholders, who received almost 1.6 Nortel shares for each BCE share. BCE retains about a 2 percent interest in Nortel. With its stock trading at a significant discount to its net asset value, BCE is a great value.

BCE and its subsidiaries are involved in the communities in which they operate. In addition to cash donations, Bell Canada makes substantial in-kind donations to various charities, including the Computers for Schools program. Through this program, companies donate computer hardware to schools in their communities and volunteer their employees' skills to help teach children to use computers.

Most of BCE's subsidiaries have employment equity policies or programs in place to encourage the hiring and promotion of people from disadvantaged groups. For example, Bell Canada modifies the workstations of visually impaired employees and provides them with information in Braille, large print, or audio tape. Three of BCE's 14 directors are women, a level of representation that is rare in corporate Canada.

BCE has faced some turmoil within its employee ranks, especially at Bell Canada where 60 percent of workers are organized under collective agreements. Union leaders have criticized management for moving ahead with workforce reductions despite registering healthy profits. In April 1999 about 9500 Bell Canada technicians and operators initiated a strike due to the sale of some operations to a U.S.-based company. BCE offers a variety of benefits to its staff, including access to an employee assistance program and university scholarships for employees' children.

Bell Canada has an environmental commitment policy and a formal environmental management and review system. The company shares its zero-waste program and system of waste audits with other companies throughout Canada. Environmental management is overseen by the social and environmental committee of the board, a rarity in the telecommunications industry. Bell Canada also produces an annual environmental report.

Bell Canada was one of 16 Canadian companies that made a commitment to eliminate their purchase of old-growth forest products and reduce their overall wood and paper consumption within three years, through the Markets Initiative. Led by a coalition of four major environmental groups—the Forest Action Network, the Friends of Clayoquot Sound, Greenpeace Canada, and the Sierra Club of B.C.— the Markets Initiative helps companies to develop environmentally sound wood and paper purchasing policies. Bell Canada's letter to the Markets Initiative said, "...it is our intention to favour those wood-based product suppliers who will have adopted sustainable practices which do not contribute to the destruction of irreplaceable natural treasures such as the ancient forests." However, Bell Canada announced its withdrawal from the program in July 2000.

BCE Inc. at a Glance

Fiscal year ended: December 31
Revenue in CDN$ millions

	1995	1996	1997	1998	1999
Total Revenue ($)	24,624	28,167	33,191	27,454	14,214
Earnings/ Share ($)	1.12	1.7	-2.53	7.07	8.35
Price to Earnings (PE)	0.36	0.51	0.9	1.93	3.6
Dividend Yield (%)	5.76	4.17	2.85	2.35	1.04

Stock Growth (High-Low-Close)

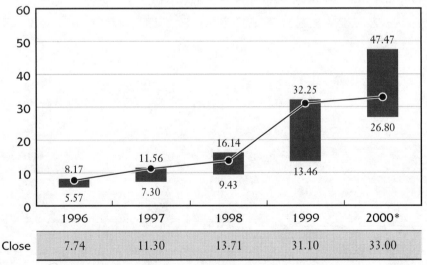

	1996	1997	1998	1999	2000*
Close	7.74	11.30	13.71	31.10	33.00

*2000 price as of August 31   Numbers reflect BCE without Nortel ownership considered.

7

BIOCHEM PHARMA INC.

275 Armand Frappier Boulevard
Laval, PQ H7V 4A7
(450) 681-1744
www.biochem-pharma.com
BCH (TSE)

CEO: Dr. Francesco Bellini
President and COO: Jacques R. LaPointe

Community	★ ★ ★
Diversity	★ ★
Employee	★ ★ ★
Environment	★ ★ ★
International Operations/ Human Rights	★ ★ ★
Product and Practices	★ ★ ★ ★

BioChem Pharma is the largest Canadian-owned biotechnology company. It is involved in the research, development, and commercialization of products used in the prevention and treatment of human diseases, including AIDS, hepatitis B (HBV), and cancer. Its most significant product is 3TC/Epivir, a drug used in association with other anti-retrovirals to treat HIV/AIDS. 3TC is licensed to Glaxo Wellcome and accounts for over US$900 million in annual sales. It is currently the leading drug in HIV/AIDS combination therapy. The same molecule has been approved for the treatment of HBV in over 30 countries and is awaiting approval in several more. Glaxo markets this product and BioChem Pharma receives significant royalties on worldwide sales. As a result of the discovery of 3TC/Epivir, the company's antiviral research team was awarded the 1996 Prix Galien Canada award for pharmaceutical research. 3TC/Epivir was recognized again in 1997 with the Prix Galien Canada award for innovative drug. 3TC/Epivir is the first product to win the Prix Galien Canada award in both categories.

BioChem Pharma is poised to expand its revenue stream with growing sales of Zeffix for HBV. A pipeline of 12 drugs and vaccines is in various stages of development. These include cancer and HIV drugs as well as alliances with Astra for non-narcotic pain drugs and with SmithKline for flu vaccines.

The company targets its donations to the scientific community, science education, and community-oriented fundraising projects. In 1997 it donated $1.1 million to Concordia University to help found a bioinformatics and biotechnology laboratory. The company grants university and college scholarships each year to students demonstrating academic excellence and innovation in health sciences.

BioChem Pharma offers its staff a comprehensive employee assistance program, including health, dental, and retirement benefits. Employees also have access to a fully equipped fitness centre, tuition and book subsidies, and professional development incentives.

BioChem Pharma has an environmental and occupational health and safety policy. Each of the company's divisions has a manager in charge of environmental issues and initiatives. BioChem Pharma's research headquarters in Laval, Quebec, is a state-of-the-art facility with various energy-conservation features built into its design. Both water and air leave the building in a more pristine condition than when they entered it, according to the company.

BioChem Pharma recycles paper and aluminum at its operations. Any radioactive waste produced through the company's research facilities is disposed of by specialized waste management companies that adhere to applicable laws and regulations. The company has implemented a $500,000 laboratory waste decontamination system at its vaccines production facilities in Massachusetts and Ste-Foy, Quebec. The system is powered by steam, and as a result requires fewer solvents and chemical products in its operation.

BioChem Pharma Inc. at a Glance

Fiscal year ended: December 31
Revenue in CDN$ millions

	1995	1996	1997	1998	1999
Total Revenue ($)	181	220	268	209	275
Earnings/ Share ($)	-0.05	0.31	0.74	1.06	1.41
Price to Earnings (PE)	N/A	109.29	41.22	40.46	19.62
Dividend Yield (%)	N/A	N/A	N/A	N/A	N/A

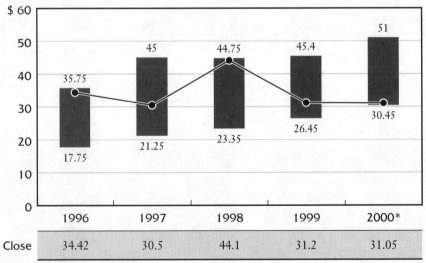

Stock Growth (High-Low-Close)

	1996	1997	1998	1999	2000*
Close	34.42	30.5	44.1	31.2	31.05

*2000 price as of August 31

8

CALPINE CORP.

50 West San Fernando Street
San Jose, CA 95113
(408) 995-5115
www.calpine.com
CPN (NYSE)

Chairman, President, and CEO: Peter Cartwright

Community	★ ★ ★
Diversity	★ ★ ★ ★
Employee	★ ★ ★ ★
Environment	★ ★ ★ ★
International Operations/ Human Rights	★ ★ ★
Product and Practices	★ ★ ★

Calpine is a fully integrated power company. The company is committed to providing its customers with low-cost and reliable electricity. Calpine was founded in 1984 to participate in the power industry when deregulation created the need for new sources of electricity. It is focused on two key technologies: combined-cycle natural gas–fired power generation and geothermal power generation. Gas-fired plants represent the fastest-growing segment of the U.S. power industry. They also represent Calpine's fastest-growing market segment.

Geothermal energy is used in areas of the world where underground heat sources are near the earth's surface. It is a niche market in many Pacific Rim countries, where commercially viable geothermal fields are prevalent. Calpine provides thermal energy for industrial customers like Phillips Petroleum and Sunsweet Growers.

Calpine's strategy is to develop highly efficient gas-fired power plants to replace aging nuclear, oil, and coal-fired plants. It also acquires power-generating facilities that meet its stringent investment criteria. The company has 44 plants in its portfolio. Calpine focuses on operating its plants as an integrated system of power generation, which allows the company to minimize costs and maximize operating efficiencies. It uses a development strategy called the Calpine Construct to build its plants. Calpine provides its own engineering, financing, construction, fuelling, and marketing services. This saved the company more than $20 million on one plant alone. Independent power producers like Calpine are positioned to benefit from continued deregulation of domestic electric power generation.

The company participates in community outreach programs at its South Point facility at the Fort Mojave Indian Reservation in Arizona.

Calpine's chief financial officer, one of five senior executives, is female. This level of diversity at the senior management level is rare in corporate America.

All of Calpine's employees are shareholders. The company's defined contribution savings plan includes a 3 percent employer profit-sharing contribution. None of Calpine's workers are covered by collective bargaining agreements, and the company has never experienced a work stoppage.

The company is a major producer of geothermal electricity, which requires minimal toxic emissions and replaces more conventional fossil and nuclear fuels. Thermal energy can be used in agricultural, residential, and industrial applications.

All of Calpine's facilities are in compliance with the U.S. *Clean Air Act* and *Clean Air Act Amendments*. The company's Aidlin geothermal plant in California and one of its steam field pipeline operations have, in certain instances, necessitated variances under applicable California air pollution control laws.

Calpine Corp. at a Glance

Fiscal year ended: December 31
Revenue in US$ millions

	1995	1996	1997	1998	1999
Total Revenue ($)	134	205	247	528	809
Earnings/ Share ($)	0.13	0.31	0.41	0.54	0.86
Price to Earnings (PE)	1.47	13.01	9.07	11.58	39.02
Dividend Yield (%)	N/A	N/A	N/A	N/A	N/A

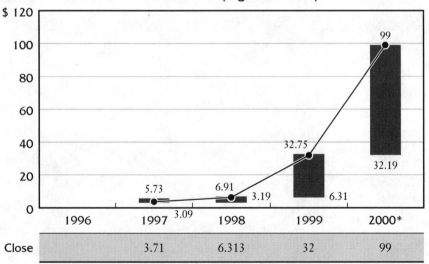

Stock Growth (High-Low-Close)

Close		3.71	6.313	32	99

*2000 price as of August 31

9
CANADIAN HYDRO
DEVELOPERS INC.

200 - 622 5th Avenue SW
Calgary, AB T2P 0M6
(403) 269-9379
www.canhydro.com
KHD (TSE)

President: John D. Keating
Senior Vice-President: J. Ross Keating

Community	★ ★ ★
Diversity	★ ★ ★ ★
Employee	★ ★ ★ ★
Environment	★ ★ ★ ★
International Operations/ Human Rights	★ ★ ★
Product and Practices	★ ★ ★

Canadian Hydro is committed to low-impact power generation. Through its 11 wind, "run-of-river" hydro, and natural gas–fired facilities in Alberta, British Columbia, and Ontario, the company generated 58.6 megawatts of electricity in 1999. With provincial and federal governments introducing emission-reduction programs and making clean air a top priority, Canadian Hydro is well positioned to take advantage of demand for zero-emission energy. Deregulation will require the power monopolies to divest of their market share and encourage development of new plants and competition within the industry. The process of deregulation is slow as most provinces adopt a wait-and-see attitude while Alberta and Ontario initiate changes. In both provinces, power will be bought and sold in a power pool, similar to trading stocks on a stock exchange. Surplus capacity is rapidly disappearing in Canada and Canadian Hydro will be there as part of the solution.

Canadian Hydro takes a "hands-on" approach during the construction of a plant and commitment to the community and environment is always at the top of its agenda. It ensures that local communities are aware of potential projects early in the planning process. For example, the company is conducting extensive public meetings with local residents, including aboriginal communities, while planning a hydro plant along Peace River in Alberta.

Ann Hughes, corporate secretary, is one of Canadian Hydro's four senior officers. This level of diversity in senior management is rare in corporate Canada.

Canadian Hydro employs about 20 people, in addition to some part-time contractors. All but two employees are shareholders through the company's stock option plan.

Approximately 18 percent of Canadian Hydro's energy production is generated through wind facilities. The company operates one of only two wind farms in Canada, on Cowley Ridge near Pincher Creek, Alberta. Wind power is a zero-emission, renewable generating technology. The Cowley Ridge facility reduces emission levels of carbon dioxide (CO_2) by 55,000 tonnes per year, sulphur dioxide by 138 tonnes per year, and nitrogen oxides by 85 tonnes per year, according to the company.

Canadian Hydro generates most of its power through run-of-river hydro plants. These facilities have a lower environmental impact than larger-scale plants because naturally flowing water is used to generate electricity, and there is little or no water storage in a headpond (storage is limited to 48 hours or less).

Wholly owned Glacier Power Ltd. is planning a run-of-river hydro plant along Peace River in Alberta. A six-metre-high weir is also planned across the river between Fairview and Spirit River. The company reports that flooding will be minimal. However, the Pembina Institute, an environmental research group, says that a 25-square-kilometre reservoir will be created covering 50 to 100 hectares of grazing land. Pembina qualifies the project as low-impact power generation but not as "green power," as described by the company.

All of Canadian Hydro's plants have been certified under Canada's Environmental Choice program as EcoLogo-certified emissions-free energy sources.

Canadian Hydro is one of 11 founding participants of KEFI-Exchange.com, Canada's first emissions trading exchange. The exchange was developed to trade CO_2 emissions reductions that occur within electricity generation as a "credit" instrument that can be used to offset emission-reduction obligations that may arise during the Kyoto compliance period. Although Canadian Hydro had not used this Internet exchange mechanism as of August 2000, the company had negotiated one bilateral deal in which it traded its reduction credits.

Canadian Hydro Developers Inc. at a Glance

Fiscal year ended: December 31

Revenue in CDN$ millions

	1995	1996	1997	1998	1999
Total Revenue ($)	3	3	5	6	9
Earnings/ Share ($)	0.03	0.02	0.03	0.01	0.05
Price to Earnings (PE)	15	34	35	75	15
Dividend Yield (%)	N/A	N/A	N/A	N/A	N/A

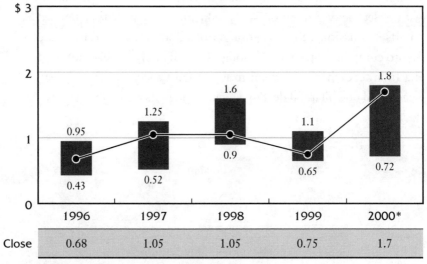

Stock Growth (High-Low-Close)

	1996	1997	1998	1999	2000*
High	0.95	1.25	1.6	1.1	1.8
Low	0.43	0.52	0.9	0.65	0.72
Close	0.68	1.05	1.05	0.75	1.7

*2000 price as of August 31

10
CANADIAN TIRE CORP.

2180 Yonge Street
Toronto, ON M4S 2B9
(416) 480-3660
www.canadiantire.ca
CTR.A (TSE)

President and CEO: Wayne C. Sales

Community	★ ★ ★
Diversity	★ ★ ★ ★
Employee	★ ★ ★ ★ ★
Environment	★ ★ ★
International Operations/ Human Rights	★ ★ ★
Product and Practices	★ ★

Canadian Tire is a hardgoods retailer that supplies automotive, home, and sports and leisure products as well as other goods and services to a network of associate stores. It is also the largest independent retailer of gasoline in Canada. With over 200 new-format stores providing customers with more products, wider aisles, and better service, Canadian Tire is positioned for growth in an increasingly competitive marketplace. The company is also focusing on new business strategies such as improving information technology and e-commerce capability.

Canadian Tire has a Social Responsibility Committee of the board of directors. Through the Canadian Tire Community Environmental Award Program, the company and its associate dealers provide up to ten annual $1000 awards to projects that improve the environment in communities in which associate stores are located. Individual stores also participate in their local communities by supporting charitable, cultural, and sports organizations.

Canadian Tire has a formal employment equity policy. There are three women among the company's 16 directors, a level of representation that is rare in corporate Canada.

Canadian Tire offers its employees a deferred profit sharing plan and an employee profit sharing plan. The company puts aside 6.75 percent of pre-tax profits, subject to certain adjustments, which is then contributed to a trustee-managed investment portfolio. In fiscal 1999, Canadian Tire contributed $21.4 million. All Canadian Tire staff are eligible to participate in the company's employee share purchase plan as well. The company matches employee contributions (up to 10 percent of salary) at a 50 percent level and pays the tax on the employer contribution.

Canadian Tire has an environmental policy and, in 1998, launched an environment, health, and safety compliance audit program. Under the program, internal teams periodically audit environment, health, and safety compliance of business units. The company's environmental policy and audit program are overseen by an environmental health and safety policy committee comprised of senior officers.

Canadian Tire offers a variety of "environmentally improved" products and services, which are advertised under its "Caring for the Environment" logo. Environmental services include a used oil collection program for customers in seven provinces and collection of customers' nickel-cadmium batteries for recycling. Associate stores collect deposits on new car and marine batteries, which are then refunded when the used batteries are returned.

The company's supply chain team works to improve its management of waste such as cardboard, scrap metal, and stretch film. According to the company, the team recycled nearly 4000 tonnes of materials in fiscal 1999 that would otherwise have been sent to landfill, a 55 percent increase compared to the previous year.

Canadians are becoming increasingly concerned about buying goods made by children, prison inmates, or forced labour, or manufactured under other forms of coercion and discrimination. Canadian Tire's formal code aims to ensure that foreign suppliers abide by international human rights and labour standards. Although Canadian Tire reports that its buyers visit major offshore suppliers to audit product quality and working conditions, the company does not employ any independent monitoring or auditing mechanisms to ensure compliance with the standards of its code.

Holders of Canadian Tire's Class A shares have no voting privileges, other than electing the greater of three directors or one-fifth of the total number of directors. Corporate governance experts advocate a one-share-one-vote system and view dual-class stock structures as a concern.

Canadian Tire Corp. at a Glance

Fiscal year ended: December 31

Revenue in CDN$ millions

	1995	1996	1997	1998	1999
Total Revenue ($)	3,771	3,907	4,087	4,347	4,728
Earnings/ Share ($)	1.38	1.51	1.79	2.09	1.89
Price to Earnings (PE)	10.78	15.07	17.15	19.26	18.2
Dividend Yield (%)	2.69	1.76	1.3	0.99	1.16

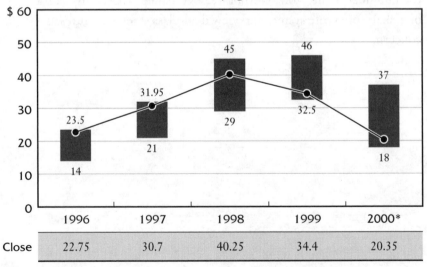

Stock Growth (High-Low-Close)

	1996	1997	1998	1999	2000*
Close	22.75	30.7	40.25	34.4	20.35

*2000 price as of August 31

11

CANWEST GLOBAL COMMUNICATIONS CORP.

3100 TD Centre
201 Portage Avenue
Winnipeg, MB R3B 3L7
(204) 956-2025
www.canwestglobal.com
CGS.S (TSE)

President and CEO: Leonard Joshua Asper

Community	★ ★ ★ ★
Diversity	★ ★ ★ ★ ★
Employee	★ ★ ★
Environment	★ ★ ★
International Operations/ Human Rights	★ ★ ★
Product and Practices	★ ★

CanWest Global Communications is an international media company. It owns and operates radio, television, and specialty cable channels in Canada, New Zealand, Australia, Ireland, and the United Kingdom. Its interactive media division and program production and distribution division operate in several countries worldwide. In July 2000

CanWest received CRTC approval to acquire WIC television assets. The deal gave the company full national coverage with four new stations in Alberta, three in B.C., and one in Ontario. To avoid too much concentration of ownership, CanWest was asked to divest its Vancouver station and WIC's Montreal station. In August 2000 the company announced the purchase of most of Hollinger's English Canada publishing assets, including a 50 percent interest in the *National Post*. This acquisition will likely double CanWest's revenue and earnings. The deal will allow CanWest to promote Internet media sites through its control of top newspapers and television stations across Canada. The company anticipates significant cost and revenue synergies as a result of these recent acquisitions.

In fiscal 1998 CanWest Global donated $1.4 million to charity, representing 1 percent of pre-tax profits averaged over the previous three fiscal years. These donations followed the creation of the CanWest Global Foundation in fiscal 1997, to which the company contributed $1 million in seed capital. The company directs the majority of its donations to the performing arts and broadcast education, particularly in Manitoba. CanWest's stations are also involved in charitable projects, including an annual fundraising telethon for the Children's Miracle Network and the provision of free airtime to numerous charitable organizations.

CanWest Global has a formal employment equity program. Three of the company's 11 directors are women, a level of representation that is rare in corporate Canada.

CanWest Global sponsors numerous awards to integrate disadvantaged groups into the industry. The Broadcaster of the Future Award for Aboriginal People, which is co-funded with the Canadian Council for Native Business, provides a four-month paid internship at the Global Television Network. The company's Scholarship Award for a Canadian with a Physical Disability combines educational funding for one year in a radio or television arts or journalism program with a summer work internship at the network. A similar award is offered to a Canadian visible minority student.

CanWest Global offers a variety of benefits to its employees, including tuition reimbursement and a service recognition program. CanWest offers all employees interest-free loans, to a maximum of 5 percent of their earnings, to purchase the company's subordinate voting shares. Employees repay the loans through payroll deductions.

Relationships between management and employees have not been cordial at some of the newspapers CanWest Global is acquiring from Hollinger Inc. Problems have included lockouts at the *Ottawa Citizen* and *Montreal Gazette* in 1996, a strike at the *St. Catharines Standard* in 1998, and a short labour dispute at two Vancouver dailies in 1999. In November 1999 the *Calgary Herald*'s editorial and distribution staff went on strike. This acrimonious conflict ended in July 2000.

CanWest Global recycles aluminum cans, glass, and paper, and separates cafeteria refuse. These initiatives are overseen by the company's internal health and safety committee.

The company issues non-voting shares, subordinate voting shares that carry one vote per share, and multiple voting shares, whose holders are entitled to ten votes per share. Corporate governance experts advocate a one-share-one-vote system and view dual-class stock structures as a concern.

CanWest Global Communications Corp. at a Glance

Fiscal year ended: August 31

Revenue in CDN$ millions

	1995	1996	1997	1998	1999
Total Revenue ($)	336	368	460	545	602
Earnings/ Share ($)	0.57	0.72	0.95	1.33	0.97
Price to Earnings (PE)	10.21	15.66	27.26	14.22	16.98
Dividend Yield (%)	N/A	0.35	0.97	1.56	1.84

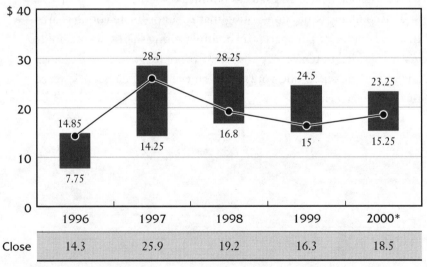

Stock Growth (High-Low-Close)

	1996	1997	1998	1999	2000*
Close	14.3	25.9	19.2	16.3	18.5

*2000 price as of August 31

12
CISCO SYSTEMS INC.

170 West Tasman Drive
San Jose, CA 95134
(408) 526-4000
www.cisco.com
CSCO (NASDAQ)

President and CEO: John T. Chambers

Community	★ ★ ★
Diversity	★ ★ ★ ★ ★
Employee	★ ★ ★ ★ ★
Environment	★ ★ ★
International Operations/ Human Rights	★ ★ ★
Product and Practices	★ ★

Cisco Systems develops and markets a complete line of routers and switching products that connect and manage communications among local and wide area computer networks. Its customers are corporations, governments, universities, and utilities worldwide. Cisco continues to benefit from the buildout of the Internet. Cisco provides key technologies to enable Internet service providers to combine voice, video, and data on a single network based on Internet Protocol. It has been acquiring companies in key areas to bring new products to an explosive market in a timely manner. Cisco has a rich valuation, but as a market leader with five-year earnings-per-share growth estimated at more than 30 percent, we believe that the valuation is justified.

During 1999 Cisco, in collaboration with the United Nations Development Program (UNDP) and two other companies, sponsored a Web site to promote poverty awareness and serve as a resource for non-profit organizations and individuals working on poverty issues. The collaboration aims to raise money to help eradicate poverty worldwide.

Through its Adopted School Program, Cisco donates cash, computer equipment, and student tutoring to schools in San Jose, Research Triangle Park, New York, and Boston. Cisco selected the schools based on their needs and the needs of their students and surrounding communities. The company has also donated technical training for vocational programs and network infrastructure to the Commercial Street Inn homeless shelter in San Jose.

In fiscal 1998 Cisco subcontracted approximately US$89 million to women-owned firms (2.3 percent of total subcontracting) and $128 million to minority-owned firms (3.4 percent).

Family-oriented benefits include flextime, a flexible spending account with a child-care option, and resource and referral services for dependent care. Employees on maternity leave receive disability pay for a period in addition to the unpaid three months of federally mandated maternity leave. Approximately 66 percent of Cisco's workforce telecommutes.

All of Cisco's non-management employees receive a quarterly cash bonus if certain company goals are met. The company distributes these bonuses based on a percentage of compensation. Bonuses typically exceed $500. The company also grants stock options to all employees when hired.

Cisco's retirement benefits are covered through a 401(k) savings plan in which it matches 100 percent of employees' contributions up to US$1500 per year. In addition, it makes discretionary contributions to the savings plan when determined by the board. It made no contribution in fiscal 1999.

In June 1999 Cisco was named in a newspaper article criticizing the labour practices of contract manufacturers that pay Asian immigrants by the piece to assemble electronics parts at home. Concerns cited included paying less than minimum wage, no overtime pay, employing children, and exposure to hazardous chemicals. These firms were subcontracted by several high-tech companies, including Cisco. Following the article, federal and California officials announced plans to launch an investigation into such practices for possible labour, tax, and safety violations. A follow-up article in October 1999 noted that Cisco conducted a review of its subcontractors and suspended contracts with four companies as a result.

Cisco's CEO received a compensation package that the company estimated at US$73.78 million in fiscal 1999, including 2.5 million stock options that the company valued at approximately US$72.83 million. In fiscal 1998 the CEO received a compensation package estimated at US$37.42 million.

The company's networking products are used to connect mainframe computers at major weapons research laboratories, including Sandia National Laboratories and Los Alamos.

Cisco Systems Inc. at a Glance

Fiscal year ended: July 31
Revenue in US$ millions

	1995	1996	1997	1998	1999
Total Revenue ($)	2,232	4,096	6,440	8,488	12,154
Earnings/ Share ($)	0.15	0.17	0.14	0.31	0.36
Price to Earnings (PE)	38.47	40.71	38.7	74.45	130.64
Dividend Yield (%)	N/A	N/A	N/A	N/A	N/A

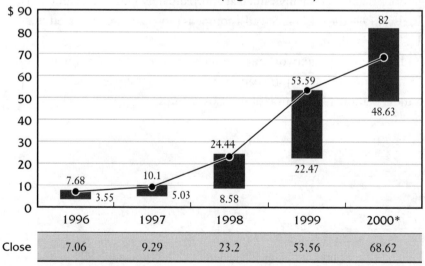

Stock Growth (High-Low-Close)

| Close | 7.06 | 9.29 | 23.2 | 53.56 | 68.62 |

*2000 price as of August 31

13

CLARICA LIFE INSURANCE CO.

227 King Street South
Waterloo, ON N2J 4C5
(519) 888-3900
www.clarica.com
CLI (TSE)

President and CEO: Robert M. Astley

Community	★ ★ ★
Diversity	★ ★ ★ ★
Employee	★ ★ ★ ★
Environment	★ ★ ★
International Operations/ Human Rights	★ ★ ★
Product and Practices	★ ★ ★

Clarica Life Insurance offers a wide range of products and services, including life and health insurance and wealth management, to over 3 million individuals and the employees of 10,000 businesses. Formerly Mutual Life of Canada, the company demutualized in July 1999. This means that it converted from a company owned by policyholders to one owned publicly by shareholders. Clarica has delivered decent earnings in nearly every business segment. The company is a potential takeover target after December 31, 2001, when takeover protection for life insurance companies is removed as part of the financial services reform.

Clarica focuses its donations on hospitals, education, and anti-violence initiatives. It is the largest corporate donor to the United Way of Kitchener-Waterloo. The company matches staff and agent contributions to United Way campaigns, in addition to other charities of their choice. Clarica has promoted the cause of organ donation since 1992, helping to identify and address the barriers to organ donation in Canada.

Clarica leases to charitable and non-profit organizations, rent-free, ten houses that it owns on a street adjacent to its head office in Waterloo. The company made the houses available to these organizations in late 1999, and is committed to leasing them for a minimum period of two years. After a community committee conducted an initial screen of applicants, Clarica employees voted to decide which tenants to accept. The organizations include the Cystic Fibrosis Foundation, Family and Children's Services of Waterloo Region, Grand River Hospital Family Hostel, and the Head Injury Association of Waterloo-Wellington.

The company has a formal statement forbidding harassment and discrimination in the workforce within its code of business conduct. Four of the company's 16 directors are women, a level of representation that is rare in corporate Canada.

Under its share purchase plan, Clarica matches 50 percent of an employee's contributions towards the purchase of company shares, up to 5 percent of an employee's target annual compensation and to a maximum of $3000 per year. Employees have access to a family services referral service, on-site fitness facilities, education subsidies, and a return-to-work program. In addition, the company has established a wellness program for all full-time and part-time employees.

At Clarica's Waterloo head office, where the majority of its staff works, employees who carpool receive a reserved, convenient parking spot. The "Green Team," a volunteer committee, explores and promotes environmentally friendly business practices throughout the company.

Clarica Life Insurance Co. at a Glance

Fiscal year ended: December 31

	1995	1996	1997	1998	1999
Total Revenue ($)	–	–	–	–	–
Earnings/ Share ($)	–	–	–	–	2.04
Price to Earnings (PE)	–	–	–	–	–
Dividend Yield (%)	–	–	–	–	0.58

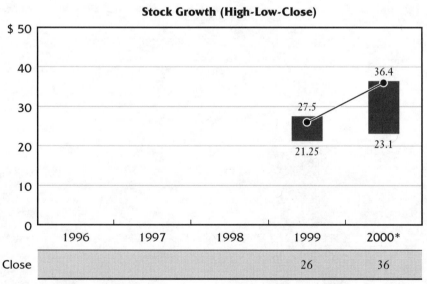

Stock Growth (High-Low-Close)

*2000 price as of August 31

14

COGNOS INC.

P.O. Box 9707, Station T
Ottawa, ON K1G 4K9
(613) 738-1440
www.cognos.com
CSN (TSE)

President and CEO: Renato Zambonini
CFO: Donnie M. Moore

Community	★ ★ ★
Diversity	★ ★ ★
Employee	★ ★ ★
Environment	★ ★ ★
International Operations/ Human Rights	★ ★ ★
Product and Practices	★ ★ ★

Cognos develops, markets, and supports software tools for enterprise application development as well as business intelligence software that allows users to access critical information through data access, reporting, analysis, and forecasting. The company's products are distributed both directly and through resellers worldwide. It has wholly owned subsidiaries operating in Australia, Belgium, Denmark, France, Germany, Italy, the Netherlands, Singapore, South Africa, Sweden,

Switzerland, and the United Kingdom. The company generated 39 percent of its fiscal 2000 revenue outside of North America. The business intelligence market continues to show strong growth and Cognos continues to emerge as a leader.

Cognos' pipeline of large deals continues to rise. The company has a strong balance sheet and in September 2000, announced the acquisition of NoticeCast software for $15 million in cash and stock. The deal will be slightly dilutive in the first year. This acquisition should strengthen Cognos' market position by adding wireless real time event notification capabilities to the company's existing technology suite.

Cognos directs charitable donations to four areas: health and welfare, education, culture, and community. The company created an employee volunteer committee and a corporate volunteerism program in 1996. During 1998 employees volunteered almost 800 hours of community service. Activities included cleaning a city park "adopted" by Cognos, craft activities at a children's festival, food drives, and a winter clothes campaign.

Cognos has a formal employment equity policy and a sexual harassment policy. One of the company's eight senior officers is female, and there is one woman on its eight-member board of directors. To help its staff balance work and family responsibilities, Cognos allows flextime scheduling and "teleworking" on a case-by-case basis.

Cognos's employee stock purchase plan is open to all permanent full-time and part-time employees of the company and its subsidiaries. The purchase price per share is 90 percent of the TSE average closing price on either the first five trading days or the last five trading days during the purchase period, whichever is less. Cognos offers a variety of benefits to its workers, including a tuition reimbursement program. At the company's head office, various lunchtime activities are available, including aerobics and martial arts classes.

Cognos undertakes regular environmental audits of its facilities, including assessments of air quality. The company has eliminated hydrofluorocarbons from the chillers and heating system at its head office in Ottawa, which is the only facility the company owns.

In May 2000 Business Objects S.A. filed an action against Cognos in the U.S. District Court for the Northern District of California for an alleged patent infringement. Cognos claims that the complaint is without merit.

Cognos Inc. at a Glance

Fiscal year ended: December 31

Revenue in CDN$ millions

	1995	1996	1997	1998	1999
Total Revenue ($)	168	208	270	342	450
Earnings/ Share ($)	0.15	0.29	0.54	0.52	1
Price to Earnings (PE)	43.35	38.58	26.32	25.79	34.99
Dividend Yield (%)	N/A	N/A	N/A	N/A	N/A

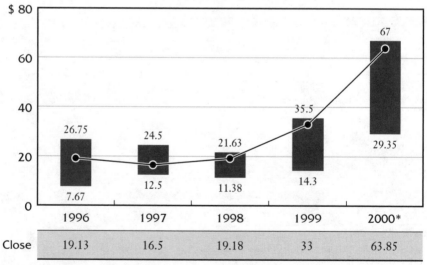

Stock Growth (High-Low-Close)

Close	19.13	16.5	19.18	33	63.85

*2000 price as of August 31

15

CREO PRODUCTS INC.

3700 Gilmore Way
Burnaby, BC V5G 4M1
(604) 451-2700
www.creo.com
CRE (TSE); CREO (NASDAQ)

CEO: Amos Michelson
President: Daniel Gelbart

Community	★ ★ ★
Diversity	★ ★ ★
Employee	★ ★ ★ ★ ★
Environment	★ ★ ★
International Operations/ Human Rights	★ ★ ★
Product and Practices	★ ★ ★

Creo Products focuses on the application of imaging and information technology. This Vancouver-based company develops, manufactures, and distributes computer-to-plate digital solutions. Creo's solutions automate the pre-press phase of commercial printing, in which master printing plates are created prior to actual printing. Its technology transfers digitized text, graphic images, and line artwork from desktop computer publishing systems directly onto printing plates.

In April 2000 Creo acquired certain preprint and print-on-demand assets of Israeli-based Scitex Corporation Ltd. to create CreoScitex, now Creo's principal operating division. The merger with Scitex is very positive for Creo shareholders, particularly since it provides the aggressive product developer with a surplus of 200 research and development engineers. It comes as no surprise that Creo will deploy the engineers to develop new products. The company has had strong revenue performance, largely due to continued strength in demand for computer-to-plate hardware and software in North America and Europe. Even Asia has been showing some interest.

The company matches employee donations to registered charitable organizations to a maximum of 3 percent of the contributing individual's salary per calendar year.

Although Creo does not have an employment equity policy, some employees are involved as volunteer mentors at local organizations that encourage women to pursue high-technology or nontraditional careers. On occasion, the company has donated money to these groups to help fund events. To help staff balance family and work responsibilities, Creo allows employees to choose their working hours in consultation with their "teams."

Creo maintains a profit sharing plan for all employees who have worked at the company for three consecutive months. All workers share equally in three-quarters of any amount set aside, while the balance is distributed at the discretion of the board of directors. In addition, all permanent Creo employees receive stock options annually. The number of options granted depends on the contribution an employee makes to the company, which is determined through a peer review process.

Creo provides its staff with comprehensive benefits, including a registered retirement savings plan towards which the company contributes

5 percent of each employee's gross salary. The company has a computer purchase program through which it matches employee contributions towards the purchase of a home computer. The company also covers the total cost of work-related training programs.

Creo has an environmental policy and an environmental management system. The company reports that it follows many of the practices of the ISO 14001 standard and that it has its products tested for electrical emissions and laser safety.

Creo Products Inc. at a Glance

Fiscal year ended: September 30

Revenue in CDN$ millions

	1995	1996	1997	1998	1999
Total Revenue ($)	–	–	130	186	268
Earnings/ Share ($)	–	–	0.33	0.59	0.89
Price to Earnings (PE)	–	–	–	–	–
Dividend Yield (%)	–	–	–	–	–

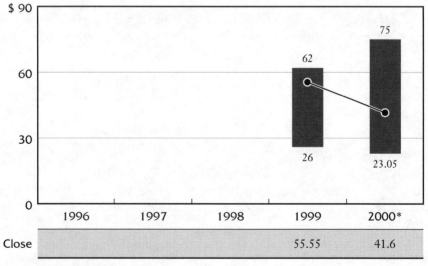

Stock Growth (High-Low-Close)

	1996	1997	1998	1999	2000*
Close				55.55	41.6

*2000 price as of August 31

16
ELECTROLUX AB

SE-105 45 Stockholm
Sweden
46-8-738-60-03
www.electrolux.com
ELUX (NASDAQ)

President and CEO: Michael Treschow

Community	★ ★ ★
Diversity	★ ★ ★
Employee	★ ★ ★
Environment	★ ★ ★ ★ ★
International Operations/ Human Rights	★ ★ ★
Product and Practices	★ ★ ★ ★

Based in Sweden, Electrolux is the world's largest household appliance manufacturer, with leading positions in various industrial, commercial, and outdoor products as well.

Electrolux was the primary sponsor of the UNICEF campaign "one drop of water," which promoted the drilling of wells in Namibia. The company supports an orphanage in Latvia for disabled children.

Electrolux is attempting to create a management profile that better reflects its geographical spread, personnel, and customer base.

Currently, a disproportionate ratio of Electrolux's executives hail from Italy, Sweden, and the United States, where the company has had operations for many years. Although 32 percent of the company's workforce is female, there is only one woman on each of the 15-member executive management team and the 10-member board of directors.

During 1998 Electrolux employed about 94,000 workers worldwide, a decrease of approximately 6 percent from the previous year, primarily due to restructuring throughout the European operations. Some labour unions have criticized the company for downsizing despite being profitable. Electrolux University conducts programs in leadership, strategic development, project management and quality control, team building, and cross-cultural communication.

Electrolux has a strong environmental profile. President and CEO Michael Treschow has said, "I believe in responsible and environmentally conscious conduct, and I subscribe to the view that a proactive environment strategy is essential to strengthen us in a competitive market...." Environmental issues are fully integrated with business activities and primary responsibility for implementation lies with environmental coordinators in the company's business sectors. The company publishes extensive environmental information on its Web site and is among the 23 Pilot Test Enterprises for the Global Reporting Initiative.

By the end of 1999, 40 production facilities had certified their environmental management systems according to the ISO 14001 standard, while 30 additional facilities had begun the certification process. Electrolux developed a set of Environmental Performance Indicators (EPI) to highlight the link between environmental work and business results and to monitor and assess its performance. EPI analysis showed that in fiscal 1999, products with the best environmental performance accounted for 21 percent of sales and 31 percent of profits.

Electrolux has undertaken numerous initiatives to reduce energy and water consumption, minimize waste, and replace hazardous substances with less-hazardous alternatives. In 1999 the recycling of waste increased by 33 percent to 329,045 tonnes from 246,488 tonnes the year before. The company reduced emissions of volatile hydrocarbons to 453 tonnes from 2065 tonnes between 1996 and 1999 by altering the painting process.

Electrolux is a leader in terms of resource-efficient appliances. In 1993 Electrolux introduced CFC-free refrigerators, the first in Europe. Since 1995 none of the company's refrigerators and freezers in Europe have contained any substances that can damage the ozone layer. In March 1997 the company launched the first line of refrigerators on the Brazilian market with no ozone-depleting potential. During 1999 both CFCs and HCFCs were entirely phased out of production in China.

Since the start of Electrolux's refurbishment project in Sweden in 1999, more than 4000 damaged or used appliances that otherwise would have been scrapped have been refurbished and sold back to the market. Similar projects are in operation in North America and England.

Electrolux has an informal human rights policy. The company has a long tradition of respecting the rights of union representatives at all of its operating units.

Electrolux AB at a Glance

Fiscal year ended: December 31

Revenue in US$ millions

	1995	1996	1997	1998	1999
Total Revenue ($)	17,393	16,147	14,278	14,505	14,037
Earnings/ Share ($)	2.25	1.49	0.24	1.34	1.34
Price to Earnings (PE)	–	–	114.6	12.89	18.77
Dividend Yield (%)	–	–	2.27	1.79	1.49

*Total Revenue and Earnings per Share figures converted from Swedish krona

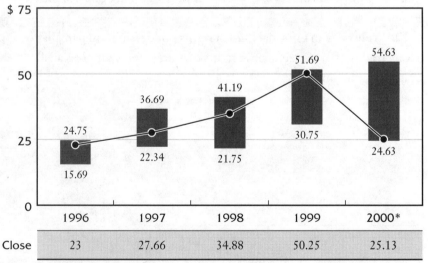

Stock Growth (High-Low-Close)

Close	23	27.66	34.88	50.25	25.13

*2000 price as of August 31

17

FAIRFAX FINANCIAL HOLDINGS INC.

Suite 800, 95 Wellington Street West
Toronto, ON M5J 2N7
(416) 367-4941
www.fairfax.ca
FFH (TSE)

Chairman and CEO: V. Prem Watsa
Vice-President and CFO: Trevor Ambridge

Community	★ ★ ★ ★
Diversity	★ ★ ★
Employee	★ ★ ★ ★
Environment	★ ★ ★
International Operations/ Human Rights	★ ★ ★
Product and Practices	★ ★

Fairfax Financial Holdings Limited is a financial services holding company that, through its subsidiaries, is engaged in property, casualty, and life insurance and reinsurance; investment management; and insurance claims management. The company is diversified across 12 business segments and has operations in 7 countries. The combined subsidiaries rank in the top 25 reinsurers in the world. At this writing, Fairfax Financial was trading at historically low valuations as a result of poor underwriting performance as measured by its combined ratio (premiums/claim losses). The company has used the decline in stock price as an opportunity to buy back stock (5 percent in 1999 alone). Investment management is a big part of the story in this industry segment, and Fairfax Financial has a solid track record in this area. Another major strength is management's commitment to shareholder value. Fairfax Financial has a target return-on-equity (ROE) of 20 percent, which it has achieved in all but 2 of the past 20 years. With the company trading close to its book value, we don't see a lot of downside for Fairfax Financial, and the upside may be considerable for long-term investors.

In fiscal 1998 and fiscal 1999, Fairfax Financial donated $7.7 million in cash to charity, representing more than 1 percent of pre-tax profits during that period. Fairfax Financial funded 60 scholarships for university and community college education in Canada in 1999.

Fairfax Financial and its operating companies have employment equity policies. The company and its subsidiaries have a variety of programs in place at their operations to help employees balance work and family responsibilities, including job sharing and flextime options.

Fairfax Financial's cash profit sharing plan is open to all employees. Through this plan, a percentage of profits is distributed to employees, based in part on their individual performance and position at the company, provided that the company meets certain underwriting targets. The company reports that it has made distributions to all employees through the plan in each of the last five years. It also maintains a share purchase plan to encourage directors, officers, and employees to acquire subordinate voting shares. The company contributes 30 cents for every dollar contributed by the staff member. If Fairfax Financial achieves at least a 20 percent return on equity, it will contribute another 20 cents.

Fairfax Financial's chairman and CEO owns 100 percent of the company's multiple voting shares (ten votes per share) and 0.4 percent of its subordinate voting shares (one vote per share), representing approximately 55.6 percent of the total votes. Corporate governance experts advocate a one-share-one-vote system and view dual-class stock structures as a concern.

Fairfax Financial Holdings Ltd. at a Glance

Fiscal year ended: December 31

Revenue in CDN$ millions

	1995	1996	1997	1998	1999
Total Revenue ($)	1,073	1,475	2,088	3,574	5,788
Earnings/ Share ($)	9.79	15.36	21.59	32.63	9.2
Price to Earnings (PE)	10.01	18.88	14.82	16.55	26.68
Dividend Yield (%)	N/A	N/A	N/A	N/A	N/A

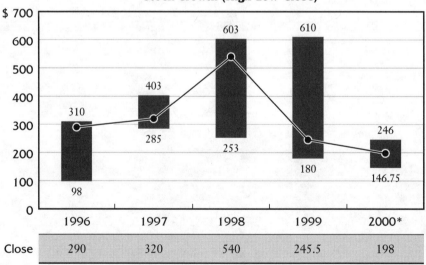

Stock Growth (High-Low-Close)

Close	290	320	540	245.5	198
	1996	1997	1998	1999	2000*

*2000 price as of August 31

18

FANNIE MAE

3900 Wisconsin Avenue NW
Washington, DC 20016-2892
(202) 752-7115
www.fanniemae.com
FNM (NYSE)

Chairman and CEO: Franklin D. Raines
Vice-Chairman and COO: Daniel Mudd

Community	★ ★ ★ ★ ★
Diversity	★ ★ ★ ★ ★
Employee	★ ★ ★
Environment	★ ★ ★
International Operations/ Human Rights	★ ★ ★
Product and Practices	★ ★ ★ ★

The Federal National Mortgage Association, affectionately known as Fannie Mae, is a U.S. government–sponsored company (a quasi-agency) that provides liquidity to home mortgage markets by buying mortgages from lending institutions. If it keeps the mortgages in its portfolio, it profits from the difference between what it pays to borrow and what it earns on the loans. Because of its quasi-agency status, Fannie

Mae has access to low cost financing, which gives it a significant competitive advantage. If Fannie Mae sells the loans to investors as mortgage-backed securities, it receives about 0.2 percent in return for guaranteeing payment of principal and interest. Fannie Mae has good long-term growth prospects, and has delivered record operating profits in every quarter for the past 12 years.

The Fannie Mae Foundation is one of few corporate foundations to make program-related investments, which it does through its Community and Neighborhood Development Fund. As of December 1998 the Fannie Mae Foundation had approximately US$15.5 million in below-market-rate loans outstanding to community development organizations throughout the U.S.

Fannie Mae provides diversity training to all employees and integrates diversity issues into all aspects of its in-house training and development courses. It has a standing diversity council and an office of diversity. Fannie Mae incorporates diversity issues into its calculations for executive incentive pay. Fannie Mae's CEO and board chair is African American. Two women and two minority members (including the CEO) sit among the ranks of the company's eight senior executives, while three women and three minority members (including the CEO) serve on the company's 16-member board of directors. This level of diversity at the senior management and board levels is rare in corporate America.

Fannie Mae offers a variety of programs to help its staff balance work and family responsibilities. Family leave is 24 weeks, double the federally mandated allotment, sometimes with full pay. The company offers four weeks' paid paternity leave, phase-back for new mothers, research and referral services, and adoption aid. Its work–life initiatives include flexible work schedules, extended bereavement leave, and leave for parents to volunteer at their children's schools. Alternative work schedules include flextime, compressed workweeks, job sharing, and telecommuting.

Staff benefits at Fannie Mae include free annual health assessments for employees and their partners, unlimited financial assistance for business-related undergraduate or graduate degrees, on-site learning and study centres, job rotation programs, and stipends for commuters who use mass transit. Through its Employer Assisted Housing Program, the company also offers a housing loan to employees with two or more years of service. Fannie Mae forgives a portion of the loan, which can be up to 7 percent of the property's value, with each subsequent year of employment.

In June 1999 the company announced an initiative to test and develop mortgage financing products that allow homeowners to take advantage of "green building" methods. The initiative, in partnership with the National Association of Home Builders, will also include a US$100 million investment by Fannie Mae in environmental product initiatives.

As a secondary source for mortgages for low- to moderate-income households, Fannie Mae's basic product benefits the economically disadvantaged. In March 2000 Fannie Mae announced a program through which it will underwrite US$2 trillion in new mortgages for women, woman-headed families, and young families over the next ten years.

Fannie Mae at a Glance

Fiscal year ended: December 31

Revenue in US$ millions

	1995	1996	1997	1998	1999
Total Revenue ($)	22,250	25,054	27,776	31,498	36,968
Earnings/ Share ($)	1.95	2.48	2.83	3.23	3.72
Price to Earnings (PE)	15.8	15.05	20.16	22.7	16.78
Dividend Yield (%)	2.2	2.02	1.47	1.3	1.73

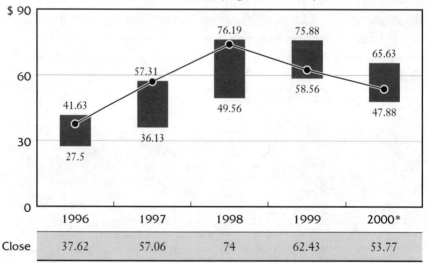

Stock Growth (High-Low-Close)

	1996	1997	1998	1999	2000*
Close	37.62	57.06	74	62.43	53.77

*2000 price as of August 31

19
GAIAM INC.

Suite 300, 360 Interlocken Boulevard
Broomfield, CO 80021
(303) 222-3600
www.gaiam.com
GAIA (NASDAQ)

Chairman and CEO: Jirka Rysavy

Community	★ ★ ★
Diversity	★ ★ ★ ★ ★
Employee	★ ★ ★ ★
Environment	★ ★ ★
International Operations/ Human Rights	★ ★ ★
Product and Practices	★ ★ ★

Gaiam provides goods, services, and information to customers in five market segments: sustainable economy, healthy living, alternative health care, personal development, and ecological lifestyles. The company has named this industry "LOHAS," an acronym for Lifestyles of Health and Sustainability. Through its Web site, catalogues, television, and 15,000 retail points, Gaiam offers products and services such as yoga and meditation instructional materials and products, natural health instructional materials, and products for total well-being.

Gaiam supports the Arbor Day Foundation and Rain Forest Rescue to plant trees and purchase rain forest acreage that is in jeopardy of being developed. In the last few years, the company has planted more than 30,000 trees and preserved more than 22 hectares of rain forest. Gaiam's donations are based on its annual corporate paper usage. On a local level, Gaiam is involved with Habitat for Humanity, Stream Clean Up, and Community Food Share as well as a variety of fundraising walks and runs. It donates inventory and product samples to local non-profit organizations for fundraising auctions.

Two of the company's four senior executives are women. Lynn Powers is president and COO and Janet Matthews is CFO. Powers and one other woman serve on the company's five-member board of directors. This level of diversity at the senior management and board levels is rare in corporate America.

Gaiam offered stock options grants to all employees prior to the company's initial public offering in 1999. The company's 150 employees are eligible to participate in the Long-Term Incentive Plan, which provides for the granting of options to purchase shares of the company's common stock. Gaiam offers its employees a US$1000 per person annual tuition payment plan.

Gaiam's marketing material is printed on 60 percent recycled paper, including 30 percent post-consumer. The company ships all of its products in boxes made with post-consumer recycled fibre content. Gaiam uses vegetable-based, water-soluble, and environmentally friendly packing "peanuts" that can be composted or will dissolve when water is added, in addition to clean waste paper collected from local sources, to pack its products.

In fiscal 1999 the company's CEO received a total compensation package estimated at US$481,000, notably low for companies followed by Kinder, Lydenberg, Domini & Co., Inc., an American social investment research firm.

In September 1998 Gaiam created two classes of common stock. The Class B common stock is owned entirely by the company's founder and CEO and is restricted as to its sale or transfer. Each share of Class A common stock is entitled to one vote, while each share of Class B common stock is entitled to ten votes. Corporate governance experts advocate a one-share-one-vote system and view dual-class stock structures as a concern.

Gaiam Inc. at a Glance

Fiscal year ended: December 31

Revenue in US$ millions

	1995	1996	1997	1998	1999
Total Revenue ($)	–	–	19	30	45
Earnings/ Share ($)	–	–	0.08	0.11	0.19
Price to Earnings (PE)	–	–	–	–	88.19
Dividend Yield (%)	–	–	N/A	N/A	N/A

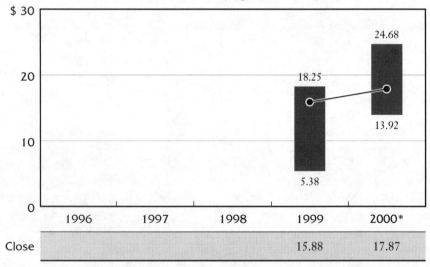

Stock Growth (High-Low-Close)

	1996	1997	1998	1999	2000*
Close				15.88	17.87

*2000 price as of August 31

20

GENNUM CORP.

P.O. Box 489, Station A
Burlington, ON L7R 3Y3
(905) 632-2996
www.gennum.com
GND (TSE)

President and CEO: Ian L. McWalter

Community	★ ★ ★
Diversity	★ ★ ★
Employee	★ ★ ★ ★ ★
Environment	★ ★ ★
International Operations/ Human Rights	★ ★ ★
Product and Practices	★ ★ ★

Gennum Corporation designs, manufactures, and markets electronic components, primarily silicon integrated circuits and thick-film hybrid circuits. The company's products include low-voltage audio electronic amplifiers and analog signal processing circuitry for the hearing instrument industry, video signal distribution and processing components for the professional video and broadcast television markets, and user-specific integrated circuits for a variety of specific applications. In June 2000 Gennum announced that it was reorganizing the company along the lines of business to allow it to focus on the needs of each of its business units. It created separate divisions for video products and hearing instrument products. The company plans to increase its research and development efforts in the near future. Gennum has significant cash resources and no debt.

The company directs its charitable donations towards education, health and welfare, culture, and the environment.

According to a Gennum spokesperson, the company has a published values document and reviews its employment systems to ensure that no discriminatory barriers to employment, promotion, or retention exist. However, none of the company's eight senior officers or seven directors is female.

All permanent, full-time Gennum employees participate in the company's incentive compensation plan. The amount paid to employees is a function of their salary, level of responsibility, and the company's rate of return on net assets. For officers, the calculation is based on salary, responsibility, and Gennum's rate of return on equity. Gennum pays the incentive amount in cash to approximately 50 percent of its employees (those at lower levels of responsibility). For the remainder, a proportion of the incentive is paid in Gennum shares, with this proportion increasing with greater levels of responsibility.

All staff members are eligible to participate in Gennum's employee stock purchase plan, to which they may contribute up to 5 percent of base salary. The company contributes 50 cents per dollar of employee contributions.

Gennum's environmental policy outlines the company's commitment to respond proactively to protect the environment, minimize risk, and meet or exceed statutory requirements. The company performs soil, air, and waste water audits as required.

In September 1999 Gennum opened an 8826-square-metre manufacturing, research, and development facility located in Burlington,

Ontario. The complex includes "clean rooms," a high-purity water system, high-purity gas systems, and a waste acid neutralizer. The company has eliminated the use of chlorofluorocarbons (CFCs) in the manufacture of its products.

Gennum Corp. at a Glance

Fiscal year ended: November 30
Revenue in CDN$ millions

	1995	1996	1997	1998	1999
Total Revenue ($)	42	53	61	83	93
Earnings/ Share ($)	0.19	0.27	0.33	0.45	0.49
Price to Earnings (PE)	16.76	29.82	29.95	34.49	39.66
Dividend Yield (%)	1.32	0.63	0.63	0.49	0.49

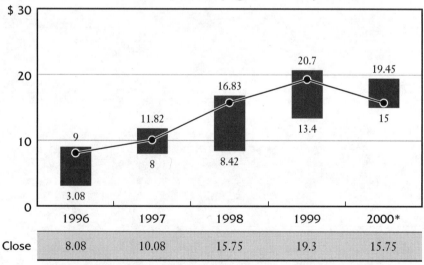

Stock Growth (High-Low-Close)

	1996	1997	1998	1999	2000*
Close	8.08	10.08	15.75	19.3	15.75

*2000 price as of August 31

21
G.T.C. TRANSCONTINENTAL GROUP LTD.

Bureau 3315, 1 Place Ville Marie
Montreal, PQ H3B 3N2
(514) 954-4000
http://transcontinental-gtc.com
GRT.A (TSE)

Chairman, President, and CEO: Remi Marcoux

Community	★ ★ ★
Diversity	★ ★ ★
Employee	★ ★ ★ ★
Environment	★ ★ ★ ★
International Operations/ Human Rights	★ ★ ★
Product and Practices	★ ★

G.T.C. Transcontinental Group's printing division includes pre-press, printing, and finishing plants in Canada, the U.S., and Mexico. Its technology division manufactures digital audio CDs, CD-ROMs, and DVDs, while the distribution division delivers flyers and other advertising material to homes in Manitoba, Ontario, and Quebec. The publishing group is Quebec's leading producer of specialized business and financial publications. The company has grown rapidly but methodically in the past few years and is now the second-largest commercial printer in Canada. Growing technology and e-commerce initiatives should help G.T.C. continue to increase its revenue and profits. A growth rate of over 15 percent combined with low price-to-earnings and price-to-book ratios make this an undervalued company with good upside potential.

G.T.C.'s donations program focuses on the arts, education, and health. In addition to its cash donations, the company donates printing services to charitable causes.

Ten of the company's plants have profit sharing plans, through which workers receive a percentage of profits beyond a pre-established threshold. The amount is shared between office and production employees, either equally or in proportion to their pay. The decision to introduce the profit sharing scheme into other facilities rests with local management and employees.

G.T.C. offers a variety of benefits to its staff, including a comprehensive employee assistance program, family services referral, tuition subsidies, and management and employee training programs. In 1999 the company created its own Awards for Excellence to recognize employees whose initiatives have significantly improved the company's operations and/or its relationships with customers.

G.T.C. adopted a comprehensive environmental policy in 1993. The company also prepared an environmental handbook for each printing plant and held a series of information and training sessions for employees. Over the past few years, each printing plant has conducted an environmental audit of its operations.

Opened in 1994, G.T.C.'s Vancouver web printing plant is the first such facility in the world at which there are no waste pipes or drains in production areas and where most liquid waste is recycled. The process uses recycled paper, reuses over 90 percent of all inks and solvents, and uses vegetable-based oils and inks in printing. G.T.C., along with its partners, developed and installed a complete membrane technology system through which all water and process chemistry is treated at the molecular level and then reused within the facility. The company estimates that, in total, more than 13.6 million litres of waste liquid will be eliminated through these technologies. The plant has received EcoLogo certification under the federal government's Environmental Choice Program.

G.T.C. installed a new solvent recovery system at its Owen Sound, Ontario, facility in 1997, which enables the plant to recover 90 percent of the 50,000 litres of solvent used annually. At the Brampton, Ontario, printing plant, a closed-loop water cooling system conserves fresh water and has reduced energy requirements by 40 percent. The plant has also eliminated harmful rubber-based glues from the binding process and replaced them with non-toxic, water-based alternatives.

Holders of the company's Class A common shares are entitled to one vote per share, while Class B shareholders are entitled to 20 votes per share. Class A shares will be converted to Class B shares if an offer is made for the company. Corporate governance experts advocate a one-share-one-vote system and view dual-class stock structures as a concern.

G.T.C. Transcontinental Group Ltd. at a Glance

Fiscal year ended: December 31

Revenue in CDN$ millions

	1995	1996	1997	1998	1999
Total Revenue ($)	960	1,045	1,124	1,336	1,548
Earnings/ Share ($)	0.73	0.06	0.87	1.05	1.22
Price to Earnings (PE)	14.73	166.67	13.46	14.33	15.7
Dividend Yield (%)	1.12	1.2	0.98	1.06	0.84

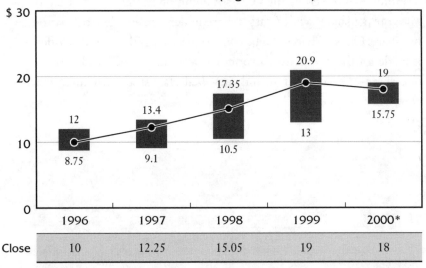

Stock Growth (High-Low-Close)

	1996	1997	1998	1999	2000*
Close	10	12.25	15.05	19	18

*2000 price as of August 31

22
HAIN CELESTIAL GROUP INC.

50 Charles Lindbergh Boulevard
Uniondale, NY 11553
(516) 237-6200
www.thehainfoodgroup.com
HAIN (NASDAQ)

President, CEO, and Founder: Irwin D. Simon

Community	★ ★ ★
Diversity	★ ★ ★ ★
Employee	★ ★ ★
Environment	★ ★ ★
International Operations/ Human Rights	★ ★ ★
Product and Practices	★ ★ ★ ★

Hain Celestial Group was formed from the merger in 2000 of Hain Food Group, a leading natural, organic, and specialty food company, and Celestial Seasonings, a market leader in specialty teas. In 1998 Hain acquired four natural food companies from the Shansby Group and others, as well as the Nile Spice Soup and Meal Cup business from Quaker Oats. In September 1999 Hain formed a strategic alliance with

H.J. Heinz to produce natural and organic foods and soy beverages. Hain's strategy calls for continued growth through mergers and acquisitions, investing in brands and consumer awareness, outsourcing manufacturing, and developing export opportunities in the rapidly growing natural food market.

CEO, Irwin Simon, reports that the company's priority has been the effective integration and consolidation of businesses and operations in order to be well positioned to capitalize on the growth of their brands going forward. The subsequent repositioning of Celestial Seasonings to focus on brand strength and changes to business operations are expected to contribute positively to Hain Celestial's performance in fiscal 2001.

Women in senior executive positions include Ellen B. Deutsch, executive vice-president of the grocery and mass market division. One woman and one minority member serve on the company's nine-member board of directors. This level of diversity at the board level is rare in corporate America.

Hain Celestial Group has acquired several businesses during the past several years, leading to a significant increase in the total number of employees. Certain hourly workers at the company's Health Valley facility have elected to be represented by the Bakery, Confectionery and Tobacco Workers' Union. The company (and its predecessor) has been engaged in negotiations with the union since November 1997; however, no agreement has been reached.

In December 1994 Hain Celestial Group adopted its Long-Term Incentive and Stock Award Plan, which provides for the granting of incentive stock options to employees, directors, and consultants.

The company has not experienced any environmental regulatory problems in the past and has not been subject to any fines or penalties.

Hain Celestial Group markets natural and organic quality food products. Natural foods are foods that are minimally processed, largely or completely free of artificial ingredients, preservatives, and other non-naturally occurring chemicals, and as near to their whole, natural state as possible. Organic foods are typically those that have been grown without the use of toxic and persistent chemicals, thereby lessening the amount of pesticide residues in food, as well as in soil and groundwater. The company has stated that it will ensure that the foods it markets are free of genetic modification.

Hain Celestial Inc. at a Glance

Fiscal year ended: June 30
Revenue in US$ millions

	1995	1996	1997	1998	1999
Total Revenue ($)	58	68	65	104	205
Earnings/ Share ($)	0.28	0.24	0.12	0.28	0.71
Price to Earnings (PE)	13.02	16.07	51.04	47.17	25.72
Dividend Yield (%)	N/A	N/A	N/A	N/A	N/A

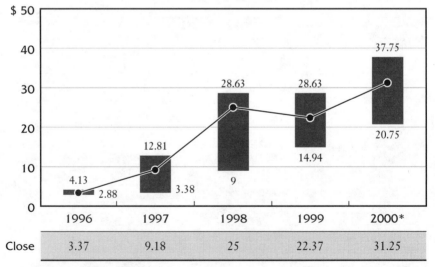

Stock Growth (High-Low-Close)

Close	3.37	9.18	25	22.37	31.25

*2000 price as of August 31

23

HEWLETT-PACKARD CO.

3000 Hanover Street
Palo Alto, CA 94304
(650) 857-1501
www.hp.com
HWP (NYSE)

President and CEO: Carleton S. Fiorina

Community	★ ★ ★ ★
Diversity	★ ★ ★ ★ ★
Employee	★ ★ ★ ★
Environment	★ ★ ★
International Operations/ Human Rights	★ ★ ★
Product and Practices	★ ★ ★

Hewlett-Packard is a leading manufacturer of computer products and services, including laser and inkjet printers, scanners, copiers, faxes, personal computers, servers, and workstations. The company has focused on computing systems, imaging and printing systems, and information technology services. It has stated that leveraging the power of the Internet will be the basis for its new product rollouts.

The company's Diversity in Education Initiative focuses on improving math and science education and encouraging women and minorities to enter technical occupations. It also supports K–12 mathematics and science enrichment programs that increase the pool of minority members, women, and persons with disabilities pursuing technical careers, and university programs that increase retention rates of women and minority students in engineering and science.

In June 1999 Hewlett-Packard named Ms. Carleton S. Fiorina as its president and CEO. Two women (including the CEO) serve among the company's six senior executives. In fiscal 1998 women accounted for 28 percent of Hewlett-Packard's officers and managers, and minorities accounted for 15 percent. This level of diversity at the senior management level is rare in corporate America and is due largely to Hewlett-Packard's Accelerated Development diversity program, through which it provides mentoring to women and minorities in middle management.

Hewlett-Packard's family benefits include 52 weeks of maternity leave, 40 weeks more than is federally required. The company offers resource and referral services, phaseback for new mothers, and adoption aid of US$2500. Alternative work schedules include flextime (used by over 50 percent of employees), compressed workweeks, job sharing, and telecommuting.

Hewlett-Packard is the only large U.S.-based computer firm with a full employment philosophy to have avoided large-scale layoffs in the 1990s. In difficult times it has reduced all salaries by 10 percent rather than lay off staff. Hewlett-Packard distributes 12 percent of pre-tax profits to eligible employees on a semi-annual basis through its cash profit sharing plan.

Hewlett-Packard has developed a set of guidelines to introduce environmentally sound practices into the full product development and manufacturing process. Its managers are held personally accountable for the environmental performance of their work sites.

In the U.S., between 1988 and 1995 Hewlett-Packard reduced by 99.9 percent the release of chemicals targeted under the Environmental

Protection Agency's (EPA's) 33/50 voluntary emissions reduction program. During the same period, the company reduced all reportable toxic-air emissions by 98 percent, and all reportable chemical releases by 91 percent. Between 1990 and 1995 Hewlett-Packard reduced hazardous wastes generated at its manufacturing facilities worldwide by 23 percent.

In October 1998 Hewlett-Packard announced that it had funded the successful development of an environmentally beneficial way to clean silicon wafers. The method uses carbon dioxide under high pressure and temperature to clean the wafers, thereby eliminating the need for solvents.

In December 1998 Hewlett-Packard was one of more than 20 corporations that pledged to phase out the use and sale of products from trees harvested from old-growth forests. The project commits the companies to conduct an internal audit and to stop purchasing or using materials derived from old-growth timber.

The EPA alleges that Hewlett-Packard violated the U.S. *Toxic Substances Control Act* by failing to inform the EPA of its use of a toxic printer-ink chemical. The EPA is seeking US$2.5 million in fines.

Hewlett-Packard manufactures mini-supercomputers, supercomputers, and computer workstations for the U.S. Department of Defense. Supercomputers are used for nuclear weapons research. The company's Convex Computer subsidiary manufactures mini-supercomputers, some of which have defence applications.

Hewlett-Packard Co. at a Glance

Fiscal year ended: October 31

Revenue in US$ millions

	1995	1996	1997	1998	1999
Total Revenue ($)	31,519	38,420	42,895	39,419	42,370
Earnings/ Share ($)	2.32	2.46	2.95	2.77	3.34
Price to Earnings (PE)	14.12	15.47	16.5	18.9	29.89
Dividend Yield (%)	1.15	1.17	1.11	1.16	0.72

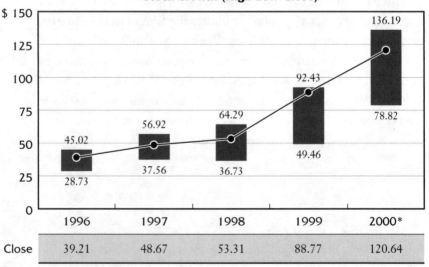

Stock Growth (High-Low-Close)

	1996	1997	1998	1999	2000*
Close	39.21	48.67	53.31	88.77	120.64

*2000 price as of August 31

24
HUSKY INJECTION MOLDING SYSTEMS LTD.

500 Queen Street South
Bolton, ON L7E 5S5
(905) 951-5000
www.husky.ca
HKY (TSE)

President and CEO: Robert Schad

Community	★ ★ ★ ★
Diversity	★ ★ ★
Employee	★ ★ ★ ★ ★
Environment	★ ★ ★ ★
International Operations/ Human Rights	★ ★ ★
Product and Practices	★ ★ ★

Husky Injection Molding Systems designs and manufactures injection molding equipment, including machines, molds for polyethylene terephthalate (PET) preforms, hot runners, and robots. Customers use Husky's equipment to manufacture a wide range of products, such as soft drink and water bottles, auto components, cellphones, and laptop computers. Husky is a world leader in PET preform molding presses, serving customers in 70 countries. Overcapacity in the PET market made 1999 a slow year for Husky after several years of nearly 20 percent revenue growth (compared to 5 to 6 percent for the plastics machinery sector overall). Overall, though, Husky is a world-class company, and as the overcapacity in the PET market is eliminated by new applications and increased consumption, that value will be recognized by the market.

Husky donates 5 percent of pre-tax profits to charitable organizations. This level of giving is outstanding and extremely rare in corporate Canada. The Schad Foundation directs 50 percent of the company's charitable budget, primarily in support of environmental projects. The other half is divided among Husky locations worldwide in support of local community and educational initiatives.

Husky has a formal employment equity policy, which includes targets to increase the representation of women, aboriginal people, members of visible minority communities, and persons with disabilities at all levels of the company. The Bolton, Ontario, manufacturing facility and head office has an on-site child development and daycare facility.

All full-time Husky employees participate in the company's bonus plan. Bonuses are based on Husky's profitability and the performance of each employee's business unit. All full-time and permanent part-time employees can participate in the company's share purchase plan.

Employees at Husky's Bolton operation have access to a medical doctor, a naturopathic doctor, a chiropractor, massage therapists, a physiotherapist, and an occupational health and safety nurse. Its subsidized cafeterias emphasize healthy eating, as healthy foods are less expensive than higher-fat alternatives.

Husky's environmental, health, and safety policy commits the company to incorporate environmental considerations into its business strategy and planning. The company has also committed to certify all of its business units to the ISO 14001 Environmental Management System Standard.

Husky's buildings incorporate precast wall sections and argon-filled windows, both with high insulation values; motion sensors to activate lighting; and energy-efficient motors and hand dryers. Its central chilling units are designed to use free winter cooling, and all new refrigerants must have zero global-warming or ozone-depletion potentials. The company has naturalized its landscaping, eliminating the use of herbicides, pesticides, chemical fertilizers, and gas mowers.

Husky's waste minimization program led to a landfill diversion rate of 93 percent. Between 1997 and 1999 the company eliminated annual use of 246,025 litres of trichloroethane by converting solvent-based metal part cleaners to water-based washers, stopped using more than 4000 litres of toluene and naphtha annually, and eliminated the annual release of 8.4 tonnes of volatile organic compounds by converting its painting process to water-based coatings.

Husky participates in the federal Voluntary Challenge and Registry, a national program that calls on Canadian companies, governments, and organizations to voluntarily submit action plans to help stabilize Canada's net emissions of greenhouse gases (GHG) at 1990 levels by the year 2000. Despite Husky's efforts, its GHG emissions rose from 7346 tonnes of carbon dioxide equivalent in 1990 to 23,283 tonnes by 1998, an increase of 217 percent. Husky has committed to stabilizing net GHG emissions at 1990 levels by 2005.

Husky Injection Molding Systems Inc. at a Glance

Fiscal year ended: July 31
Revenue in CDN$ millions

	1995	1996	1997	1998	1999
Total Revenue ($)	–	–	856	1,087	1,069
Earnings/ Share ($)	–	–	–	–	0.21
Price to Earnings (PE)	–	–	–	–	140.63
Dividend Yield (%)	–	–	–	–	N/A

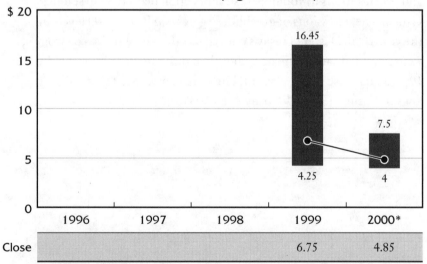

Stock Growth (High-Low-Close)

	1996	1997	1998	1999	2000*
Close				6.75	4.85

*2000 price as of August 31

25

INTEL CORP.

2200 Mission College Boulevard
Santa Clara, CA 95052-8119
(408) 765-8080
www.intel.com
INTC (NASDAQ)

President and CEO: Dr. Craig R. Barrett

Community	★ ★ ★
Diversity	★ ★ ★ ★ ★
Employee	★ ★ ★ ★ ★
Environment	★ ★ ★ ★ ★
International Operations/ Human Rights	★ ★ ★
Product and Practices	★ ★

Intel is the world's largest maker of microprocessors, the central processing units of PCs. Intel designs, develops, manufactures, and markets the Pentium family of microprocessors. The chip industry has been through a number of boom and bust cycles as manufacturers have struggled to keep supply and demand in balance. The proliferation of the Internet and the increasing use of semiconductors in cell phones and other equipment will fuel growth in this sector. As the market leader, Intel is well positioned to benefit from that growth.

Intel's 1998 donations included grants for academic research, scholarships for women seeking engineering degrees, and support for primary and secondary school education. The company also donated almost US$59.5 million in equipment to various educational institutions. In 1994 and 1995 Intel was involved in a controversy with a coalition of community groups in New Mexico, headed by the SouthWest Organizing Project (SWOP), over its plans to expand its manufacturing facility in Rio Rancho. Although Intel and SWOP announced various agreements in August 1996, SWOP has expressed a number of continuing reservations.

Intel has a nondiscriminatory employment policy and provides diversity training. At many of its facilities, Intel offers work-family benefits, including job sharing, telecommuting, and child-care resource and referral. The facilities in Israel and Malaysia offer on-site child care.

Intel offers cash profit sharing to substantially all employees through cash bonus and employee bonus programs. In February 1997 Intel announced that all employees would be eligible for at least 50 stock options. To encourage ride sharing and alternative forms of transportation, Intel offers preferential parking for carpools, provides subsidies for transit passes, and maintains facilities for cyclists.

Intel applies the same environmental standards to its facilities worldwide. Its comprehensive annual environmental report details a variety of company-wide efforts to improve its impact on the environment

Computer chip manufacturers require a significant amount of water, primarily to create the ultra-pure water necessary to remove impurities from chips during production. The amount of water used by Intel facilities is a matter of controversy in a number of communities, particularly in Albuquerque because of its desert ecology. Intel reports that from 1997 to 1998 the company's use of water in manufacturing worldwide declined 14 percent.

In 1998 Intel recycled 58 and 42 percent of its chemical waste in the U.S. and worldwide, respectively. That year, emissions of nitrogen oxide and carbon monoxide increased from the previous year. Aggregate emissions of volatile organic compounds decreased slightly from 1997.

Intel works with more than 1000 suppliers and subcontractors in the U.S. territories, East Asia, Southeast Asia, Central America, Western Europe, and the Middle East. Intel's code of conduct sets forth the company's expectations and minimum standards for suppliers and sub-contractors, and addresses child labour, freedom of association/collective bargaining, sanitation, lighting and ventilation, and safety. The company routinely verifies compliance with the code.

In March 1999 Intel settled antitrust charges filed by the Federal Trade Commission (FTC), alleging that Intel stifled innovation and competition by retaliating against firms that sought to enforce patents. The FTC agreed to drop its charges, while Intel agreed to allow customers with whom it has patent disputes access to design data.

Intel had a US$45 million contract through 2000 to provide support for a supercomputer to be operated at Sandia National Laboratories in Albuquerque. The computer simulates and studies nuclear weapons to monitor their reliability and safety. Intel has also had supercomputer contracts with Oak Ridge National Laboratory in Tennessee. Both laboratories have been major centres of nuclear weapons research.

Intel Corp. at a Glance

Fiscal year ended: December 31
Revenue in US$ millions

	1995	1996	1997	1998	1999
Total Revenue ($)	16,202	20,847	25,070	26,273	29,389
Earnings/ Share ($)	0.5	0.73	0.97	0.86	1.05
Price to Earnings (PE)	14.05	22.58	18.11	33.49	35.63
Dividend Yield (%)	0.25	0.14	0.16	0.11	0.13

Stock Growth (High-Low-Close)

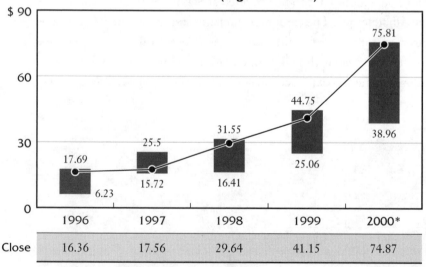

	1996	1997	1998	1999	2000*
Close	16.36	17.56	29.64	41.15	74.87

*2000 price as of August 31

26

INTERFACE INC.

Suite 2000, 2859 Paces Ferry Road
Atlanta, GA 30339
(770) 437-6800
www.ifsia.com
IFSIA (NASDAQ)

Chairman, President, and CEO: Ray C. Anderson

Community	★ ★ ★
Diversity	★ ★ ★ ★
Employee	★ ★ ★ ★
Environment	★ ★ ★ ★ ★
International Operations/ Human Rights	★ ★ ★
Product and Practices	★ ★ ★

With annual sales of over US$1 billion, Interface is a world leader in the commercial and institutional interiors industry. It sells products and services in more than 110 countries and provides 40 percent of the commercial carpet tile purchased worldwide. The company will begin production of a new commercially viable, biodegradable carpet product manufactured from polylactic acid (PLA), a renewable resource derived from corn. PLA was developed through a joint venture between Dow, a leading chemical company, and Cargill, the world's largest agricultural products company. Interface estimates that plant-derived products could make up as much as 10 percent of its business over the next three years. In addition to carpet tile, Interface products and services include broadloom carpet, vinyl flooring, upholstery fabrics, furniture services, leasing, and flooring installation, maintenance, and reclamation. It also offers services designed to enhance the workplace through experiential learning and organizational development.

The company's charitable programs focus on environmental education, including support for the well-being of indigenous populations.

Two women, one of whom is a member of a visible minority, serve on the company's 13-member board of directors. This level of diversity at the board level is rare in corporate America.

Interface is committed to developing and maintaining an enthusiastic and collaborative workforce. It offers on-the-job General Equivalency Diploma (G.E.D.) programs, foreign-language classes, and American citizenship classes to all U.S. employees. In Canada, the flooring operation subsidizes energy conservation audits and retrofits for employees' homes.

Interface is a signatory to the CERES Principles. Many of the company's manufacturing facilities are ISO 14001 certified. Some of the world's leading authorities on global ecology serve as consultants to the company, including Paul Hawken, author of *The Ecology of Commerce*. Interface publishes a "sustainability" report biannually.

Interface urges its suppliers to apply sustainability standards to their own businesses. The company says it will increase its contracts with those suppliers that make environmental improvements and terminate contracts with those who do not.

Interface pioneered the modular carpet concept in 1973. Under its new sustainability initiative, the company has developed the concept further to include maintenance, removal, and recycling of the carpet it installs.

In late 1994 Interface began a long-range program called EcoSense, which was designed for the company to achieve greater resource efficiency and ultimately achieve ecological sustainability. The company's goal is to no longer be a net "taker" from the earth. The program's key elements are closed loop recycling, using benign sources of energy for production processes, and eliminating wasted raw materials and energy from all operations.

Interface initiated a worldwide war-on-waste program in 1995, which consists of multidisciplinary groups of employees identifying and eliminating waste from processes or products. The company reports that it saved approximately US$90 million eliminating such waste between 1995 and 1998.

In 1996 Interface began its ReEntry program, in which materials from old carpets are broken down and used again as raw materials rather than placed in landfills. A year later the company introduced a carpet product, Terratex, that is made entirely from 100 percent recycled polyester fibre.

Interface introduced a new flooring product in 1999 called Solenium, which can be completely remanufactured by separating the product into its component materials and then remaking it into an identical new product. The Rocky Mountain Institute estimates that Solenium's manufacturing process, combined with the company's service lease, reduces by 97 percent the materials and energy involved in the production, upkeep, and disposal of normal broadloom carpet.

Interface Inc. at a Glance

Fiscal year ended: December 31

Revenue in US$ millions

	1995	1996	1997	1998	1999
Total Revenue ($)	802	1,002	1,135	1,281	1,228
Earnings/ Share ($)	0.41	0.6	0.76	0.56	0.45
Price to Earnings (PE)	16.67	16.77	18.83	10.55	13.07
Dividend Yield (%)	1.41	1.22	0.93	1.78	3.13

Stock Growth (High-Low-Close)

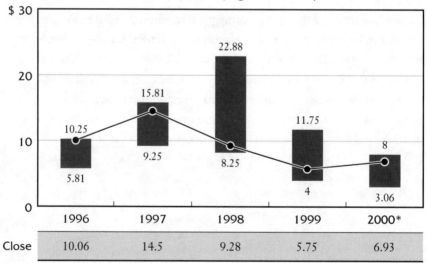

Close	10.06	14.5	9.28	5.75	6.93

*2000 price as of August 31

27

INVESTORS GROUP INC.

One Canada Centre
447 Portage Avenue
Winnipeg, MB R3C 3B6
(204) 956-8532
www.investorsgroup.com
IGI (TSE)

President and CEO: H. Sanford Riley

Community	★ ★ ★ ★
Diversity	★ ★ ★ ★
Employee	★ ★ ★ ★
Environment	★ ★ ★
International Operations/ Human Rights	★ ★ ★
Product and Practices	★ ★ ★ ★

Investors Group is a financial services company that offers a wide range of products and services from 100 financial planning centres across Canada. It is the country's largest manager and distributor of mutual funds, with over $40 billion in assets under management. Investors Group has retained and attracted new assets by offering its customers third-party funds managed by companies like AGF and Fidelity. It has recently pursued alternative distribution strategies with the formation of Scudder Maxxum, which distributes the exclusive JANUS product line. Investors Group continues to raise its dividend while posting earnings growth above 20 percent.

Between fiscal 1997 and 1999, Investors Group donated about $6.6 million in cash to charities through its Community Investment Program, representing 1 percent of pre-tax profits. It provides donations primarily to charities involved in education and youth development, arts and culture, and sports. Through its Community Service Support Program, for example, Investors Group encourages employee community participation by providing grants to charitable organizations with which its employees and representatives are involved as volunteers. The company also matches employee donations to such charitable organizations through its Matching Gift Program.

Investors Group conducts training on diversity awareness, sponsors educational courses and seminars specifically for women, and conducts employee surveys on how to increase the role of women in management. The company has a partnership with the University of Manitoba through which up to five positions in the university's Certificate Program in Management Development for Women are reserved for female employees of Investors Group. As part of its Working Together for Success program, Investors Group's employees have access to personal and educational leaves of absence, nontraditional work arrangements such as job sharing and working at home, and a maternity leave "top-up" program.

Investors Group matches 50 percent of employee contributions for the purchase of company stock. Approximately 77 percent of eligible employees participate in this program. The company also offers a variety of benefits to its employees, including an employee assistance plan and tuition subsidies.

The company has implemented a variety of environmental initiatives, including recycling programs for paper and aluminum cans, company mugs, and monthly draws for a transit pass or bus tickets. It also issues an environment credit card. The company donates a percentage of the fees earned from the card to environmental groups or to projects selected by cardholders.

The SUMMA mutual fund, launched in 1986 and one of 52 mutual funds in the Investors Group family, is managed in accordance with a set of social and environmental screening criteria. These criteria prohibit investment in companies involved in the production of alcohol, pornography, weapons, gambling, or tobacco. They also exclude companies that are closely associated with repressive regimes, or that have failed to adopt and administer effective pollution controls or protection policies.

Investors Group Inc. at a Glance

Fiscal year ended: December 31

Revenue in CDN$ millions

	1995	1996	1997	1998	1999
Total Revenue ($)	579	687	843	974	1,048
Earnings/ Share ($)	0.46	0.56	0.7	0.89	1.12
Price to Earnings (PE)	17.97	24.37	32.22	29.63	18.39
Dividend Yield (%)	2.23	1.81	1.33	1.44	2.38

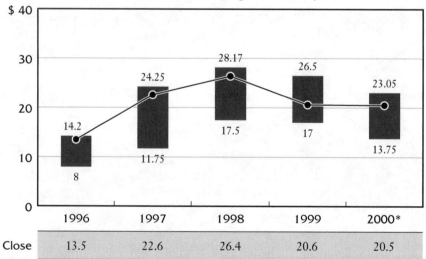

Stock Growth (High-Low-Close)

	1996	1997	1998	1999	2000*
Close	13.5	22.6	26.4	20.6	20.5

*2000 price as of August 31

28

JDS UNIPHASE CANADA LTD.

1 Antarres Road
Nepean, ON K2E 8C4
(613) 727-1303
www.jdsunph.com
JDU (TSE); JDSU (NASDAQ)

Co-Chairman and CEO: Jozef Straus
President and COO: Charles J. Abbe

Community	★ ★ ★
Diversity	★ ★ ★
Employee	★ ★ ★
Environment	★ ★ ★
International Operations/ Human Rights	★ ★ ★
Product and Practices	★ ★ ★

JDS Uniphase Canada Ltd. is a wholly owned subsidiary of JDS Uniphase Corporation. JDS Uniphase Canada Ltd.'s shares are listed on the Toronto Stock Exchange; they are economically equivalent to, and may be exchanged for, common shares of JDS Uniphase Corporation. JDS Uniphase manufactures and distributes active fibre optic components and modules for use in the telecommunications industry, including cable television providers.

JDS Uniphase has emerged as the largest component and subsystem supplier in the optical networking industry. This is one of the fastest growing segments of communications as telecommunications service providers are transitioning their networks from electrical to optical technologies in an attempt to meet growing bandwidth requirements. More bandwidth means that more information can be sent in less time. Studies have shown that demand for bandwidth may increase by as much as 200 times in the next three years.

JDS Uniphase has moved into a leadership position in supplying optical components through product innovation, aggressive mergers and acquisitions, manufacturing expertise, and the industry's broadest product portfolio. JDS Uniphase has also developed strong working relationships with its customers. This is a major strength in a market where new designs require extensive qualification periods.

We expect a continued explosion in data traffic to provide a healthy backdrop for optical component market growth over the next several years. Industry pundits predict that this market will grow in excess of 40 percent annually. In anticipation of this demand, JDS Uniphase is considering doubling or tripling its existing manufacturing capacity within the next 12 to 18 months. The stock price is high but seems justified given the high sales and earnings-per-share growth rates.

Outside of Canada and the United States, JDS Uniphase has operations in Australia, the Netherlands, Switzerland, and the United Kingdom. Most salaried workers at the company's operations in Germany and the Netherlands are represented by collective agreements. To date, these facilities have not experienced any work stoppages.

JDS Uniphase is required to comply with employment equity legislation in the United States. Employees at JDS Uniphase may purchase common shares in the company through its employee stock purchase plan. Under the plan, shares are purchased through regular payroll deductions. Employees based in the United States may opt into a 401(k) salary deferral plan, through which they may contribute up to $10,000 of their salary annually. In turn, the company matches 25 cents per dollar contributed by employees who have at least six months of service.

JDS Uniphase Canada Ltd. at a Glance

Fiscal year ended: June 30

Revenue in US$ millions

	1995	1996	1997	1998	1999
Total Revenue ($)	42	69	106	185	282
Earnings/ Share ($)	0	0.01	-0.07	-0.07	-0.54
Price to Earnings (PE)	115.32	150	54.44	65.45	375.15
Dividend Yield (%)	N/A	N/A	N/A	N/A	N/A

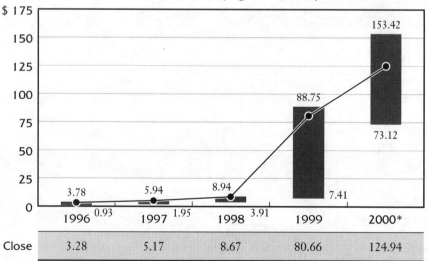

Stock Growth (High-Low-Close)

Close	3.28	5.17	8.67	80.66	124.94

*2000 price (in U.S. dollars) as of August 31

29

THE JEAN COUTU GROUP (PJC) INC.

530 Beriault Street
Longueuil, PQ J4G 1S8
(450) 646-9611
www.jeancoutu.com
PJC.A (TSE)

Chairman and CEO: Jean Coutu
President and COO: François Jean Coutu

Community	★ ★ ★ ★
Diversity	★ ★ ★ ★ ★
Employee	★ ★ ★
Environment	★ ★ ★
International Operations/ Human Rights	★ ★ ★
Product and Practices	★ ★

The Jean Coutu Group is one of North America's largest distributors
and retailers of pharmaceutical and parapharmaceutical products. In
Canada the company operates PJC Jean Coutu and Maxi Drug franchises and PJC Clinic stores. In the United States the company operates Brooks pharmacies. Alongside Shoppers Drug Mart and London

Drugs, Jean Coutu has been a leader in adopting aggressive marketing strategies that focus on health and beauty aids, home products, convenience foods, and other front-of-store merchandise to counter decreasing pharmacy margins. Customers can also order prescription refills via telephone and the Internet.

In fiscal 1998 the company donated $912,000 to charity, or 1.2 percent of pre-tax profits. This was an increase from the $812,000 donated in the previous year, representing 1.4 percent of pre-tax profits. The company's donations focus on education as well as social and public health issues.

Four of the company's 16 directors are female, a level of representation that is rare in corporate Canada.

In 1993 the company's head office opened its first on-site daycare, which is equipped to handle 60 children, from newborns to five-year-olds. The company also offers flextime arrangements to help employees balance work and family responsibilities.

The company is in the process of introducing a participatory management scheme at each of its franchises. Under this structure, employees elect internal boards to facilitate dialogue between staff and management. The company provides franchisees with a team of consultants to assist in introducing the program. As of the end of fiscal 1998 50 franchisees had introduced the management model.

The company offers a variety of benefits , including tuition subsidies, access to a corporate sports complex, and a comprehensive employee assistance program. Through this program, the company offers workers and their family members free and confidential personal, legal, and professional counselling.

The company has implemented an environmental policy for all Canadian operations. In fiscal 1998 the company formed an environmental committee to explore ways to improve its environmental performance.

At the company's head office, paper, cardboard, old computers, and used ink cartridges are salvaged for recycling. Most of the company's products are packaged in reusable plastic containers or recycled cardboard boxes. Broken wooden pallets are also salvaged.

At its Canadian franchises, the company offers a salvage program for expired medications and used syringes. The company also encourages franchisees to recycle paper, cardboard, and empty film containers. Environmental guidelines are included in the company's operating manual, which is updated regularly and distributed to all franchisees.

At its Canadian distribution centre, the company salvages oil and grease from its vehicles and uses biodegradable household products. During winter it uses ice-thawing products and gravel instead of calcium chloride.

In 1990 The Jean Coutu Group, along with several other drugstore chains and the Association Québécoise de Pharmaciens Propriétaires, was charged under the federal *Competition Act* for allegedly conspiring to price-fix dispensing fees for birth control pills and prescription narcotics. In May 1995 all of the defendants pleaded guilty. The parties agreed to fines totalling $2 million. As a result, company franchisees were required to pay a total of $289,500.

Holders of the company's Class A shares are entitled to one vote per share, while Class B shares provide ten votes per share. Corporate governance experts advocate a one-share-one-vote system and view dual-class stock structures as a concern.

The Jean Coutu Group (PJC) Inc. at a Glance

Fiscal year ended: May 31

Revenue in CDN$ millions

	1995	1996	1997	1998	1999
Total Revenue ($)	1,273	1,614	1,710	1,940	2,289
Earnings/ Share ($)	N/A	0.88	1.08	1.2	1.4
Price to Earnings (PE)	11.29	11	14.34	26.76	21.43
Dividend Yield (%)	0.86	1.15	0.92	0.53	0.61

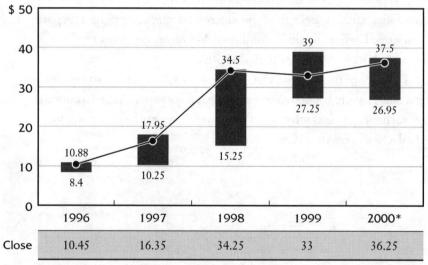

Stock Growth (High-Low-Close)

Close	1996	1997	1998	1999	2000*
	10.45	16.35	34.25	33	36.25

*2000 price as of August 31

*Earnings per Share and stock prices were formulated pre-split.

30
MEDTRONIC INC.

7000 Central Avenue NE
Minneapolis, MN 55432
(612) 514-4000
www.medtronic.com
MDT (NYSE)

Chairman and CEO: William W. George
President and COO: Arthur D. Collins, Jr.

Community	★ ★ ★ ★
Diversity	★ ★ ★ ★
Employee	★ ★ ★ ★
Environment	★ ★ ★
International Operations/ Human Rights	★ ★ ★
Product and Practices	★ ★

Medtronic is a global manufacturer of medical devices. It manufactures and markets products for medical applications, including abnormal heartbeats, and vascular and cardiac surgery. Medtronic is a leader in the cardiac stent, defibrillator, pacemaker, and other markets. It is also a leading market presence in the quickly growing neurology market, and has over 150 patents in this area. It has formed alliances with Healtheon/WebMD, IBM, and Microsoft through which it will provide new Internet-based programs to connect specialty care teams of physicians to patients with chronic cardiovascular disease. Since 1995 the company has grown both sales and earnings per share by more than 20 percent annually.

Medtronic directs most of its donations towards education with a focus on science for pre-collegiate students. In 1992 the company initiated its STAR program, which aims to improve K–12 science education and targets economically disadvantaged, female, and minority students. The Conference Board has recognized STAR as the best in its class for innovative corporate-sponsored education programs. In 1997 Medtronic announced plans to extend the program through 2000 with an additional US$3 million grant.

In fiscal 1998 Medtronic initiated charitable grants that emphasize grassroots health projects in areas outside the United States where the company has operations. In China, the company provided a US$25,000 grant to the Laubach Literacy program. It supports parent education on health practices and helps develop community health projects.

The company provides dependent care resource and referral, flex-time and job sharing, and up to 16 hours per year in unpaid time off to attend school conferences or classroom activities relating to a child's education. It offers pre-tax set-asides for dependent care and subsidizes child care for mildly sick children of employees who cannot stay home to care for them.

Medtronic's retirement options include a 401(k) profit sharing savings plan, through which the firm matches a percentage in cash of employee contributions up to 6 percent of base compensation. The company contribution depends on the firm's after-tax profits. Through its Employee Stock Ownership Plan, Medtronic allocates 2.5 to 4 percent of compensation in company stock to employee retirement accounts.

Medtronic reports that its environmental, health, and safety program has made progress in the last several years, including reduction of hazardous waste by 70 percent at the company's Promeon facility in Minnesota and reduction of lost-time incidents by 90 percent at its cardiopulmonary facility in California.

In August 1998 a Canadian couple filed a lawsuit against Medtronic on behalf of approximately 6000 Canadians who received the company's pacemaker between 1988 and 1993. The plaintiffs allege that the company knowingly marketed defective pacemakers. Medtronic also faces numerous lawsuits in the United States, but none has been certified as a class action. Plaintiffs in Canada seek US$275 million in damages.

In fiscal 1998 Medtronic's CEO received a compensation package valued at US$19.84 million, including a non-cash component consisting primarily of stock options valued at US$11.08 million.

Medtronic's policy on animal testing is aimed at reducing as far as possible within regulatory requirements the use of animals and the number of animals used for research. In the United States, manufacturers of medical devices are required by law to conduct some tests on animals. For some tests that previously used animals, the company now uses cell culture, mathematical models, and computer simulations in the preliminary phases of research.

Medtronic Inc. at a Glance

Fiscal year ended: April 30
Revenue in US$ millions

	1995	1996	1997	1998	1999
Total Revenue ($)	1,742	2,169	2,438	3,343	4,232
Earnings/ Share ($)	0.47	0.55	0.51	0.39	0.9
Price to Earnings (PE)	34.07	43.59	44.87	54.22	49.24
Dividend Yield (%)	0.42	0.47	0.39	0.32	0.4

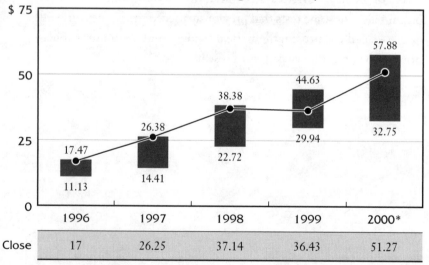

Stock Growth (High-Low-Close)

Close	17	26.25	37.14	36.43	51.27
	1996	1997	1998	1999	2000*

*2000 price as of August 31

31

MICROSOFT

One Microsoft Way
Redmond, WA 98052-6399
(425) 882-8080
www.microsoft.com
MSFT (NASDAQ)

Chairman and Chief Software Officer: Bill Gates
President and CEO: Steve Balmer

Community	★ ★ ★ ★
Diversity	★ ★ ★ ★ ★
Employee	★ ★ ★ ★
Environment	★ ★ ★
International Operations/ Human Rights	★ ★ ★
Product and Practices	★ ★

Microsoft develops and markets operating systems, applications software, hardware, and manuals for PCs, as well as Internet and intranet software and technologies. It is the world's largest software company and has positioned itself to become the leading provider of software and services for the Internet. Microsoft operating system software runs approximately 90 percent of the PCs currently in use. In the early

1990s it entered the business applications market with Microsoft Word and has subsequently dominated the applications software market. Revenue should continue to grow through recent product offerings.

A major focus of Microsoft's charitable giving is establishing computer services for the disadvantaged through its Equal Access program. The company also donates software to non-profit organizations. In January 2000 Microsoft, along with Intel, launched an international education program to train teachers in 20 countries to use technology in the classroom. Microsoft announced that it will contribute US$344 million in software and support.

Microsoft has a nondiscriminatory employment policy. A 1999 survey by *Careers & the disABLED* magazine ranked Microsoft first among 50 companies with a reputation for employing and accommodating the disabled.

Family benefits include adoption assistance of up to US$5,000 and four weeks of paid leave, as well as up to eight weeks unpaid maternity leave beyond the 12 weeks required by U.S. legislation.

Microsoft makes extensive use of stock options as an incentive for rank-and-file employees. More than 80 percent of Microsoft's employees receive stock options, which are granted on a discretionary basis at hiring or annual employee reviews.

Microsoft faces numerous conflicts with its long-term temporary employees. Approximately 5000 to 6000 of its 31,000 employees are now considered by the courts to be "common-law" employees. In January 2000 the U.S. Supreme Court let stand a May 1999 federal appeals court ruling that 10,000 current and former temporary employees ("permatemps") were entitled to participate in the company's discounted stock-purchase plan. Microsoft is also facing claims regarding temporary workers' rights to retirement plans, health insurance, vacation, holidays, and sick leave.

Microsoft has conservation and recycling programs at its Redmond, Washington, campus. Employees at Seattle locations reduced waste by 79 percent from 1996 to 1997 by recycling and reusing paper, toner cartridges, CD-ROMS, and software.

In fiscal 1998 and 1999 respectively Microsoft spent 17 percent ($2.46 billion) and 15 percent ($2.81 billion) of its revenue on product research and development. The company has been notably aggressive and innovative in new product development.

In May 1998 the U.S. Justice Department and 19 state attorneys general sued Microsoft, alleging that it had illegally dominated the market for computer software and had sought to extend this monopoly to the market for Internet browsers. In April 2000 the U.S. District Court of the District of Columbia ruled that Microsoft violated antitrust laws by restricting competition in the computer software market, monopolizing the Internet browser market, and illegally tying its Windows operating system to its Internet browser product. The federal government and 19 state attorneys general proposed that the company be split into two entities: one based around Microsoft's Office application software and its Internet business and the other involving its Windows operating system software. In June 2000 the court issued an order that implemented substantially all of the proposed remedies. These restrictions on Microsoft's business activities will apply while Microsoft goes through the appeals process.

Microsoft at a Glance

Fiscal year ended: June 30
Revenue in US$ millions

	1995	1996	1997	1998	1999
Total Revenue ($)	5,937	8,671	11,358	15,262	19,747
Earnings/ Share ($)	0.43	0.66	0.84	1.42	1.7
Price to Earnings (PE)	30.36	43.03	41.16	60.3	72.97
Dividend Yield (%)	N/A	N/A	N/A	N/A	N/A

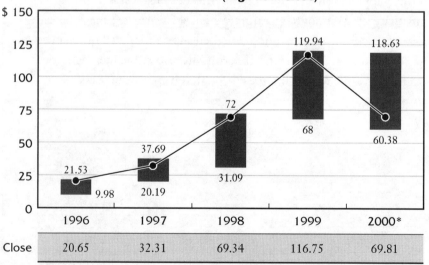

Stock Growth (High-Low-Close)

	1996	1997	1998	1999	2000*
Close	20.65	32.31	69.34	116.75	69.81

*2000 price as of August 31

32

MITEL CORP.

350 Legget Drive
Kanata, ON K2K 2W7
(613) 592-2122
www.mitel.com
MLT (TSE)

President and CEO: Kirk K. Mandy

Community	★ ★ ★
Diversity	★ ★ ★
Employee	★ ★ ★ ★
Environment	★ ★ ★
International Operations/ Human Rights	★ ★ ★
Product and Practices	★ ★ ★

Mitel Corporation is among the world's top ten telecommunications semiconductor manufacturers. It has state-of-the-art manufacturing facilities that support several different processes. Mitel is in a good position to become a leading provider of semiconductor components and systems for the telecommunications industry. As one of the few providers of complete public branch exchange systems, it is well positioned to offer new products to its existing customer base. Mitel's recent entry into optoelectronic and other components should give its earnings a substantial boost.

Mitel's corporate donations focus on research and education. In early 1997 the company helped establish the School of Information Technology and Engineering at the University of Ottawa.

Mitel has a formal employment equity policy. It runs a daycare referral program to help employees balance work and family responsibilities. Mitel's profit sharing program is open to all employees. It also provides a comprehensive employee assistance program.

Mitel's environmental policy commits the company to reduce the environmental impact of its operations and to manufacture energy-efficient products that are protective of the environment. Each Mitel facility conducts quarterly internal audits and periodic external compliance audits. Mitel's semiconductor hybrid operation in South Wales is certified under the ISO 14001 Environmental Management System Standard.

Mitel has eliminated the use of chlorofluorocarbons and volatile organic compounds from its manufacturing processes and repair operations.

Each of Mitel's sites maintains reuse and recycling programs. The company's facility in Kanata, Ontario, diverts 70 percent of its solid waste from landfill. In 1997 the facility and its suppliers established a "closed loop" paper-recycling program. Mitel's office paper is collected in bins and shipped to a recycling plant, where it is reprocessed and returned to the company as clean stationery.

In partnership with the city of Kanata, Mitel's headquarters made changes to its storm water drainage system to improve the quality of run-off water from a nearby business park. A detention pond, established on Mitel property, improves the quality of water that reaches the Ottawa River. The pond also helps cool the facility in the summer months by dissipating heat generated in office areas.

Mitel's Bromont, Quebec, operation reduced its consumption of deionized water by 26 percent in fiscal 1997. At the operation's new Wafer Fab facilities, the company installed high-efficiency lights, electric motors that require less power, and scrubbers that limit air emissions from production processes. The company's Järfälla, Sweden, facility uses energy from air compressors to heat tap water, while energy from production cooling systems helps warm the facility.

Outside of Canada, Mitel and its subsidiaries have manufacturing and/or research facilities in Sweden, the United Kingdom, and the United States. Mitel also has a 50 percent interest in a joint venture with Tianchi-Mitel Telecommunications Corporation in Tianjin, China, to manufacture, distribute, and service telephone-switching systems, and a 49 percent equity investment in Mitel de Mexico S.A. de C.V. According to the Canadian Lawyers Association for International Human Rights, Mitel's code of conduct for its international operations and suppliers is based on the host country's standards and includes provisions for worker health and safety and environmental protection. However, the code provides limited protection for workers' rights and contains almost no monitoring or enforcement mechanisms.

Mitel Corp. at a Glance

Fiscal year ended: March 31
Revenue in CDN$ millions

	1995	1996	1997	1998	1999
Total Revenue ($)	1,396	576	695	881	1,310
Earnings/ Share ($)	0.45	0.32	0.8	0.2	0.45
Price to Earnings (PE)	20.45	18.23	18.9	16.91	125
Dividend Yield (%)	N/A	N/A	N/A	N/A	N/A

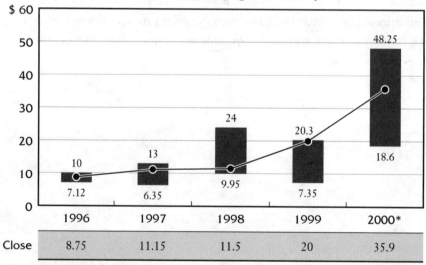

Stock Growth (High-Low-Close)

| Close | 8.75 | 11.15 | 11.5 | 20 | 35.9 |

*2000 price as of August 31

33

NOKIA CORP.

Keilalahdentie 4
P.O. Box 226
00045 Nokia Group
Finland
358-9-180-71
www.nokia.com
NOK (NYSE)

Chairman and CEO: Jorma J. Ollila
President: Pekka Ala-Pietila

Community	★ ★ ★ ★
Diversity	★ ★ ★
Employee	★ ★ ★ ★
Environment	★ ★ ★ ★
International Operations/ Human Rights	★ ★ ★ ★
Product and Practices	★ ★ ★

Finland-based Nokia is the world's leading developer and manufacturer of mobile telephone handsets as well as systems for cellular and fixed networks. It has operations in 50 countries, including a research and development facility in Canada. Nokia believes that the number of cellphone users will increase from less than 500 million to more than 1 billion by 2002.

In 1997 Nokia, Ericcson, Motorola, and Phone.com developed wireless access protocol software, designed to give cellphone users access to the Internet. The challenge for Nokia will be to maintain its leadership role in the handset market while delivering the network infrastructure to provide the high-speed data services that will move wireless technology to the next level. The company has strong, innovative management and has managed to increase its market share continuously while maintaining margins of over 20 percent. Its key competitors have margins in the low single digits.

In April 1999 Nokia donated US$1 million through the Finnish Red Cross to assist victims of the Kosovo crisis. A year later it reached an agreement with the International Youth Foundation to work to improve the lives of young people through education. During the first year of the program Nokia will invest 2.5 million Euros and focus on four countries (China, Mexico, South Africa, and the United Kingdom).

Nokia's code of conduct states that the company encourages diversity and freedom from discrimination. Ms. Sari Baldauf, president of Nokia Networks, sits on the nine-member group executive board.

Nokia has several performance-based incentive programs, including a stock option plan that covers 5000 of the company's 55,260 employees worldwide. The company paid out more than 160 million Euros based on 1999 performance through its other incentive programs. Nokia offers fitness programs and other activities to promote the well-being of its employees.

Nokia's environmental policy is based on the International Chamber of Commerce Business Charter. Nokia requires its suppliers to have an up-to-date environmental policy and management system in accordance with the ISO 14001 or another recognized standard.

At the business group and unit level, environmental initiatives are integrated into normal business activities. Each of Nokia's 21 production sites has a designated person responsible for the implementation and development of the site's environmental management system. Nokia's goal has been for these facilities to meet the requirements of ISO 14001 by the end of 2000.

In 1998 Nokia's production facilities recycled 57 percent of their total waste, including cardboard, electronic scrap, metals, paper, plastic, toner cartridges, and wood. Some sites also collected biowaste/food for composting.

Because Nokia integrates life-cycle analysis into its development, production, and marketing practices, it seeks to reduce the quantity of packaging as part of its waste management program. Improvements in packaging include abandoning the use of polyvinylchloride plastic and replacing polyurethane foam with materials based on natural fibres. The company also returns packages to its suppliers for reuse. Nokia is establishing end-of-life treatment processes for all of its products as well.

Nokia has production facilities in developing countries. Its code of conduct highlights the company's commitment to respect and promote human rights. Nokia recognizes that certain human rights should be considered fundamental and universal, and states that it will promote freedom of peaceful assembly and association as well as freedom of thought, conscience, and religion. Nokia does not use child or forced labour and does not do business with subcontractors that do so.

Nokia Corp. at a Glance

Fiscal year ended: December 31
Revenue in US$ millions

	1995	1996	1997	1998	1999
Total Revenue ($)	1,418	1,437	1,624	2,614	3,346
Earnings/ Share ($)	0.02	0.03	0.04	0.07	0.1
Price to Earnings (PE)	228.69	24.92	18.3	35.24	80.23
Dividend Yield (%)	N/A	N/A	N/A	N/A	N/A

*Total Revenue and Earnings per Share figures converted from Finnish markka

Stock Growth (High-Low-Close)

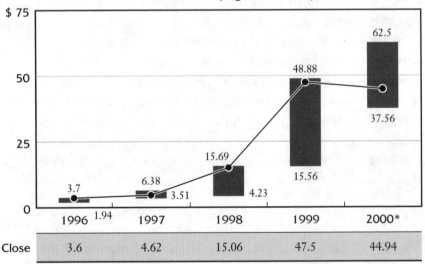

Close	3.6	4.62	15.06	47.5	44.94

*2000 price as of August 31

34

NORANDA INC.

Suite 4100, BCE Place
P.O. Box 755, 181 Bay Street
Toronto, ON M5J 2T3
(416) 982-7111
www.noranda.com
NOR (TSE)

President and CEO: David W. Kerr

Community	★ ★ ★
Diversity	★ ★ ★ ★
Employee	★ ★ ★ ★ ★
Environment	★ ★ ★ ★
International Operations/ Human Rights	★ ★ ★
Product and Practices	★ ★ ★

Noranda is an international mining and metals company, and one of the world's largest producers of zinc and nickel. After several years of less-than-spectacular results, Noranda seems poised to take advantage of increasing metal prices and improving margins. It owns 49.9 percent of Falconbridge, a base metal exploration company. Its Antamina copper mine, Bell Allard zinc and copper mine, and Magnola magnesium plant should contribute to increased earnings over the next few years. With the highest dividend yield in its group, Noranda is suitable for income investors who don't mind the cyclical nature of the resource sector.

Noranda offers on-site daycare, elder care, dependent care referral services, job sharing, and education leave to help employees balance work and family responsibilities. It also offers wellness programs, employee and family assistance programs, and health promotion plans. The company has a home computer purchase plan and awards post-secondary scholarships to employees' children.

All salaried employees at Noranda's wholly owned mining and metals operations participate in a profit sharing plan based on individual and corporate performance. All workers at these operations are eligible to participate in the employee share savings plan, under which the company matches 30 cents of every dollar contributed by the employee.

Noranda has an environmental policy and a set of sustainable development principles, through which it aims to integrate environment, health, and safety considerations into all business decisions, product development, and research activities. In 1999 it conducted 56 environmental, occupational health, industrial hygiene, and emergency response audits at its operations throughout North America and Europe. The environment, safety, and health committee of the board oversees environmental management initiatives.

Noranda received the highest grade for environmental reporting across all sectors and all countries in an analysis undertaken by the United Nations Environment Program on Corporate Reporting. It is one of two firms in the Canadian integrated mining sector to publish an environmental report, which it has done annually since 1990.

Noranda's metallurgical businesses are major recyclers of secondary copper, nickel, and precious metals. Noranda's overall sulphur dioxide emissions decreased by 65 percent between 1985 and 1999, exceeding its goal of a 57 percent reduction by the year 2002.

Despite production increases, Noranda's carbon dioxide (CO_2) emissions have remained relatively constant since 1990. The company's planned Magnolia Metallurgy magnesium plant in Danville, Quebec, will use sulphur hexafluoride (SF_6), a greenhouse gas with a global warming potential factor 24,000 times greater than that of CO_2. Although Noranda planned to begin using an alternative technology by late 2000, the company acknowledges that the use of SF_6 initially will severely compromise its greenhouse gas reduction efforts.

Noranda has a 37.5 percent interest in the Antamina copper-zinc project in Peru, which is located approximately 20 kilometres east of Huascaran National Park, a United Nations World Heritage Site. Originally the plan called for trucking concentrates through the park when production begins in 2002. In response to concerns expressed by non-governmental organizations, UNESCO, and the Peruvian government, the venture instead opted for a 302-kilometre slurry pipeline, which follows a route around the southern part of the park from the mine site to a coastal port facility. In August 1999 Huaylas and Conchucos citizens staged a 48-hour protest to voice community concerns about regional unemployment and the environmental impact of the Antamina project and another mine.

Noranda Inc. at a Glance

Fiscal year ended: December 31
Revenue in CDN$ millions

	1995	1996	1997	1998	1999
Total Revenue ($)	8,381	9,515	6,407	6,013	6,468
Earnings/ Share ($)	2.19	1.02	1	2.66	0.7
Price to Earnings (PE)	9.39	22.6	28.68	7624	27.71
Dividend Yield (%)	4.71	4.34	5.4	6.56	4.12

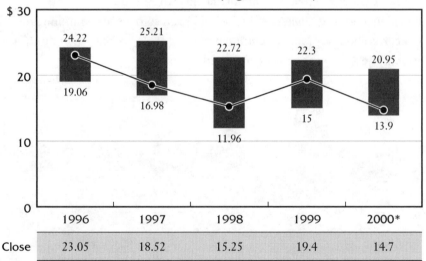

Stock Growth (High-Low-Close)

	1996	1997	1998	1999	2000*
High	24.22	25.21	22.72	22.3	20.95
Low	19.06	16.98	11.96	15	13.9
Close	23.05	18.52	15.25	19.4	14.7

*2000 price as of August 31

35

NORTEL NETWORKS CORP.

Suite 100, 8200 Dixie Road
Brampton, ON L6T 5P6
(905) 863-0000
www.nortelnetworks.com
NT (TSE)

Vice-Chairman, President, and CEO: John A. Roth

Community	★ ★ ★
Diversity	★ ★ ★
Employee	★ ★ ★ ★
Environment	★ ★ ★ ★ ★
International Operations/ Human Rights	★ ★ ★
Product and Practices	★ ★ ★

Nortel Networks is a leading global supplier of communications infra-structure equipment, including access and optical networking prod-uct lines, wireless infrastructure, and enterprise equipment. It is the second-largest supplier of telecom equipment in North America. Nortel is the clear leader in the rapidly growing optical networking market with over $5 billion in optical equipment sales in 1999. An ag-gressive acquisition strategy in the past two years has given Nortel the broadest product line of next-generation Internet products. The optical buildout and growing importance of the Internet should provide Nortel with strong earnings growth for the next few years.

Nortel is reducing its support of charities and directing the bulk of its contributions towards science, math, and technology education. The company has invested $18 million to establish the Institute in Advanced Information Technology at the University of Waterloo and the Institute in Telecommunications at the University of Toronto.

In May 1999 Nortel announced plans to sell 13 of its manufacturing plants. The Canadian Auto Workers protested the closure of the Belleville and Mississauga plants, and criticized Nortel for laying off Canadian workers when it had received millions of dollars in government grants. In November 1999 Nortel announced the creation of 5000 new positions, including 2300 at the Montreal facility and at a new plant in Kanata, Ontario.

Nortel's share purchase plan is open to all non-union employees, representing 90 percent of the workforce. Workers may contribute up to 6 percent of their salary towards the plan, which the company matches at 50 percent. Nortel also offers a range of wellness initiatives and an employee assistance program, and provides on-site fitness facilities at some locations.

Nortel's environmental management system requires all manufacturing and research facilities to conduct audits every two years. Many of the company's facilities are moving towards compliance with the ISO 14001 Environmental Management System Standard. Nortel publishes an annual environmental, health, and safety report on its Web site and engages an external auditor to ensure fair and reasonable reporting.

In 1992 Nortel became the first multinational electronics manufacturer to eliminate CFC-113 solvents from its operations worldwide. As an alternative, Nortel developed a no-clean technology for the wave soldering process, thereby reducing emissions of ozone-destroying substances by 85 percent. Prior to the changes, Nortel was Canada's single largest user of solvents containing CFCs. Nortel shared its technology through the United Nations Environment Program and the International Cooperative for Ozone Layer Protection.

Between 1993 and 1999 Nortel reduced its air emissions from manufacturing and research processes by 72 percent and its greenhouse gas emissions by 47 percent. Total pollutant releases and solid waste sent to landfill declined by 37 and 34 percent, respectively, both short of the company's goal of 50 percent.

Nortel supplied telephone switching equipment to Burma through 20-percent-owned Telrad Networks, an Israeli company. In September 2000 Nortel sold its stake in Telrad and created Nortel Networks Israel, which holds no Burmese contracts. Nortel also reports that it has obtained assurances from Telrad that "no new contracts for Nortel Networks' equipment will be entered into by Telrad in Burma." Human rights abuses by the ruling regime in Burma are among the most severe in the world.

Through its Cogent Defence Networks division, Nortel supplies many of the world's navies, armies, and air forces with specialized communications knowledge and support, including the guidance wire umbilical system for the U.K. Spearfish heavyweight torpedo. Military-related sales accounted for less than 1 percent of the company's revenue in 1998 and 1999.

Nortel Networks Corp. at a Glance

Fiscal year ended: December 31

Revenue in CDN$ millions

	1995	1996	1997	1998	1999
Total Revenue ($)	14,636	17,515	21,393	26,074	32,996
Earnings/ Share ($)	0.32	0.41	0.54	-0.37	-0.11
Price to Earnings (PE)	23.24	25.78	28.81	28.09	102.02
Dividend Yield (%)	0.99	0.8	0.63	0.58	0.15

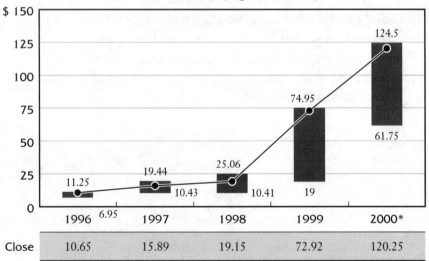

Stock Growth (High-Low-Close)

	1996	1997	1998	1999	2000*
Close	10.65	15.89	19.15	72.92	120.25

*2000 price as of August 31

36

PMC-SIERRA INC.

Suite 250, 900 East Hamilton Avenue
Campbell, CA 95008
(408) 626-2000
www.pmc-sierra.com
PMCS (NASDAQ)

Chairman, President, and CEO: Robert L. Bailey

Community	★ ★ ★
Diversity	★ ★ ★
Employee	★ ★ ★
Environment	★ ★ ★
International Operations/ Human Rights	★ ★ ★
Product and Practices	★ ★ ★

PMC-Sierra designs, develops, markets, and supports high-performance semiconductor system solutions for advanced communications markets. The company also supports non-networking customer user interface products for existing customers, but no longer develops follow-on products of this type. Expansion of the Internet, upgrading of corporate data networks, and remote access have all created the need for millions of broadband connections. This acceleration of broadband equipment deployment has benefited companies like PMC-Sierra that provide networking semiconductor devices and related technical service and support to equipment manufacturers for use in their communications and networking equipment.

PMC-Sierra's customers make broadband equipment. Time-to-market pressures have driven the outsourcing trend, and PMC-Sierra has been there with the broadest line of off-the-shelf, cutting-edge broadband semiconductor devices. PMC-Sierra's greatest challenge is growing its manufacturing capacity to meet the increasing demand for its products. The company is richly priced but its dominant position in providing silicon for the wide area network makes it a compelling investment.

As of December 1999 PMC-Sierra employed 660 people, including 376 in research and development, 100 in production and quality assurance, 110 in marketing and sales, and 74 in administration. The company continued to recruit aggressively in 2000, as its payroll swelled to more than 1100 positions. None of PMC-Sierra's senior executives or board directors is female.

PMC-Sierra offers stock option plans and an employee stock purchase plan, which it introduced in 1991. Approximately 80 percent of the company's employees are eligible to participate in the purchase plan. They may purchase a limited amount of common stock at a minimum of 85 percent of the market value at certain plan-defined dates.

PMC-Sierra management reports that money is a necessary, but not sufficient, requirement to retain and build a cohesive team. To build a strong organization, the company believes it needs a "world-changing mission that everyone can get excited about." None of PMC-Sierra's employees is represented by a collective bargaining agreement and the company has never experienced a work stoppage.

PMC-Sierra does not own or operate a wafer fabrication facility. Two outside foundries supply most of the company's semiconductor device requirements. Because PMC-Sierra contracts out its manufacturing requirements, the company reports that it does not have a formal environmental management system in place.

Subcontractors in Asia assemble all of PMC-Sierra's semiconductor products. Canadians are becoming increasingly concerned about companies that source goods made by children, by prison or forced labour, or under other forms of coercion and discrimination. PMC-Sierra does not report having a formal policy that aims to ensure that its foreign suppliers abide by international human rights and labour standards.

PMC-Sierra reports that it makes its most crucial investments in research and development. In 1999 research and development spending totalled US$60 million, a 60 percent increase from the previous year. The company planned to invest more than US$125 million in 2000. Much of this research and development activity takes place in Canada at design centres in Burnaby, Montreal, Ottawa, and Saskatoon.

PMC-Sierra Inc. at a Glance

Fiscal year ended: December 31

Revenue in US$ millions

	1995	1996	1997	1998	1999
Total Revenue ($)	188	188	127	161	262
Earnings/ Share ($)	0.01	-0.41	0.26	-0.05	0.6
Price to Earnings (PE)	27.75	18.99	30.1	55.37	190.85
Dividend Yield (%)	N/A	N/A	N/A	N/A	N/A

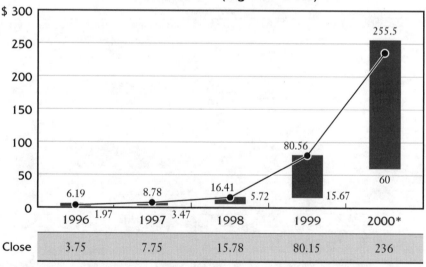

Stock Growth (High-Low-Close)

| Close | 3.75 | 7.75 | 15.78 | 80.15 | 236 |

*2000 price as of August 31

37

POLAROID CORP.

784 Memorial Drive
Cambridge, MA 02139
(781) 386-2000
www.polaroid.com
PRD (NYSE)

Chairman and CEO: Gary T. Dicamillo
Executive Vice-President and CFO: Judith G. Boynton

Community	★ ★ ★ ★ ★
Diversity	★ ★ ★ ★ ★
Employee	★ ★ ★
Environment	★ ★ ★ ★ ★
International Operations/ Human Rights	★ ★ ★
Product and Practices	★ ★ ★

Polaroid designs, manufactures, and markets instant photographic cameras, films, electronic imaging devices, and polarized filters and lenses. It is the world leader in traditional instant photography. Polaroid is focusing on product development in its faster-growing segments. It plans to revitalize its core imaging business and link its instant imaging expertise to digital imaging. Polaroid sold 400,000 digital cameras in 1999, making it a market leader. It launched more than 40 new products in 1999 and 2000. As of late 1999 Polaroid had five of the top ten selling cameras. Future earnings growth will depend on Polaroid making its cameras more profitable.

Historically Polaroid has given as much as 1.5 percent of pre-tax profits to charity, much of it to support initiatives that address women's issues. The company also gives small grants to a wide variety of community-based educational organizations. Through the company's Adopt-a-School program, employees are encouraged to spend time promoting environmental education by sharing their experiences and skills.

One of the company's five senior executives is female. This level of diversity at the senior management level is rare in corporate America. Polaroid offers subsidies for child care and elder care, job sharing, and flextime.

Almost all domestic employees receive cash bonuses tied to annual profits and paid out based on performance and salary.

Polaroid has introduced an innovative benefit for employees who are victims of domestic violence. It permits such employees to take up to two weeks off with full pay "to seek safety and protection, attend court appearances, arrange new housing, etc." The company also permits them to take up to a year off without pay and guarantees them an equivalent position when they return.

Polaroid has an employee education program, internally offering numerous courses as well as math and literacy training, and a tuition assistance program. It has offered health benefits for employees afflicted with HIV/AIDS at some of its operations since 1987. It also has comprehensive AIDS education and prevention programs.

Polaroid endorses the CERES Principles. Through its Toxic Use and Waste Reduction program, the company conducts internal audits and keeps track of environmental compliance. Plant managers must submit a report on "timely correction actions and of all excursions that occur at their facilities." Polaroid has implemented a compliance and awareness training program to educate employees about workplace safety and environmental management issues.

Polaroid's Global Sourcing Principles state that the company will do business with suppliers that "meet high health, safety, environmental, social, ethical and legal standards of performance." Polaroid periodically reviews its suppliers' waste disposal practices and ensures that materials obtained from them do not contain chlorofluorocarbons.

Between 1988 and 1996 Polaroid reduced both the use and emissions of ozone-depleting chemicals by approximately 98 percent. The company is working to reduce the emission of greenhouse gases by supporting site-based energy conservation and power plant efficiency programs.

In the late 1970s Polaroid was one of the first U.S. firms to withdraw from South Africa in response to anti-apartheid protests. In late 1994 Polaroid was among the first U.S. companies to respond to the call for foreign reinvestment by the new South African government. It announced plans to open a sales and marketing office in Johannesburg from which it would coordinate its marketing efforts throughout sub-Saharan Africa.

Polaroid Corp. at a Glance

Fiscal year ended: December 31

Revenue in US$ millions

	1995	1996	1997	1998	1999
Total Revenue ($)	2,236	2,275	2,146	1,845	1,978
Earnings/ Share ($)	-3.09	-0.9	-2.81	-1.15	0.2
Price to Earnings (PE)	82.76	23.77	22.03	22.69	16.65
Dividend Yield (%)	1.27	1.38	1.23	3.21	3.19

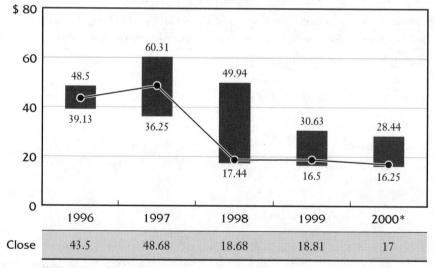

Stock Growth (High-Low-Close)

	1996	1997	1998	1999	2000*
High	48.5	60.31	49.94	30.63	28.44
Low	39.13	36.25	17.44	16.5	16.25
Close	43.5	48.68	18.68	18.81	17

*2000 price as of August 31

38

QLT INC.

887 Great Northern Way
Vancouver, BC V5T 4T5
(604) 872-7881
www.qltinc.com
QLT (TSE)

President and CEO: Dr. Julia G. Levy

Community	★ ★
Diversity	★ ★ ★ ★
Employee	★ ★ ★ ★
Environment	★ ★ ★
International Operations/ Human Rights	★ ★ ★
Product and Practices	★ ★ ★ ★

QLT Inc. is a biopharmaceutical company engaged in the research, development, and commercialization of light-activated drugs used in photodynamic therapy (PDT) for the treatment of cancer, eye disease, and other conditions. PDT is a minimally invasive procedure that requires only out-patient status or a short hospital visit. Light activates the drug to produce a toxic form of oxygen that destroys abnormal (cancer) cells. PDT is a relatively safe means of treating certain cancerous tumours near vital organs, and it has none of the significant side effects of radiation or chemotherapy.

QLT's primary product is Visudyne, a light-activated drug that treats the wet form of age-related macular degeneration (AMD). The drug received FDA approval for treating classic AMD in April 2000. There are about 500,000 new cases of wet AMD diagnosed each year, and some of these cases will require repeat treatment. Approximately 50 percent of these patients have classic AMD. QLT's research and development effort is expected to focus on expanding Visudyne's label to include early-stage AMD as well as Phase I and II trials of Verteporfin, another photosensitizer compound.

The company is also researching the use of PDT in other conditions, including cardiovascular disease. QLT has partnered with CIBA Vision to market Visudyne worldwide. Each company will receive 50 percent of profits. Launching its first major product should position QLT for rapid earnings growth over the next few years. QLT is also investing in a venture fund through a limited partnership structure. It will invest up to $25 million in equity investments over three years in exchange for R&D collaborations and the potential rights to compounds developed by the investees. This should help QLT round out the product portfolio in its pipeline.

A QLT spokesperson reports that it is not the company's policy to make corporate donations.

Three of QLT's eight senior officers are women, including Dr. Julia Levy, the company's president and CEO. This level of diversity in the senior management ranks is rare in corporate Canada. Levy is also one of seven directors.

QLT has an employee and family assistance plan and offers telecommuting options to employees to help them balance work and family responsibilities.

Through its incentive stock option plan, QLT awards options based on seniority to all employees, including those at subsidiaries, at the time of hiring and at annual reviews. The company also offers a variety of benefits to its staff, including an employee and family assistance plan. QLT's safety committee oversees health and safety matters at its operations.

QLT Inc. at a Glance

Fiscal year ended: December 31

Revenue in CDN$ millions

	1995	1996	1997	1998	1999
Total Revenue ($)	N/A	10	6	12	26
Earnings/ Share ($)	-0.38	-0.09	-0.34	-0.45	-0.55
Price to Earnings (PE)	N/A	N/A	N/A	N/A	N/A
Dividend Yield (%)	N/A	N/A	N/A	N/A	N/A

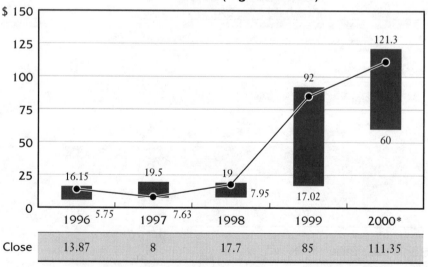

Stock Growth (High-Low-Close)

Close	13.87	8	17.7	85	111.35

*2000 price as of August 31

39

SOLECTRON CORP.

777 Gibraltar Drive
Milpitas, CA 95035
(408) 957-8500
www.solectron.com
SLR (NYSE)

Chairman, President, and CEO: Koichi Nishimura

Community	★ ★ ★
Diversity	★ ★ ★ ★ ★
Employee	★ ★ ★
Environment	★ ★ ★
International Operations/ Human Rights	★ ★ ★
Product and Practices	★ ★ ★ ★

Solectron is the world's largest provider of electronic manufacturing services (EMS) to original equipment makers (OEMs) in the computer, telecommunications, networking, and other related electronics industries. By partnering with an EMS provider, OEMs can gain access to the latest equipment, product knowledge, and manufacturing expertise without making large capital investments. Solectron provides customized, sophisticated electronic assembly and turnkey manufacturing equipment that enables OEMs to reduce their time to market. Solectron combines computer-assisted manufacturing and testing with just-in-time manufacturing, total quality control, statistical process control, and continuous flow manufacturing. Solectron is very well positioned to capitalize on the tremendous growth opportunities in this industry.

Solectron is a member of the Santa Clara Valley Manufacturing Group, which consists of executives from companies in Silicon Valley that address community problems, including transportation, housing, and education. Solectron also supports the Asian Law Alliance, an organization that provides legal counselling services to individuals who face housing, immigration, domestic violence, and civil rights problems in northern California.

Koichi Nishimura, an Asian American, is CEO, chairman, and president of Solectron. Four of the company's seven senior executives are Asian American. Two minority members, including the CEO, serve on Solectron's ten-member board of directors. This level of diversity at the senior management and board levels is rare in corporate America. Diversity at the senior levels is reflected throughout Solectron's ranks. The company reports that approximately four dozen languages and dialects are currently spoken in the workplace. It often publishes information sheets for employees in six languages.

Solectron has a worldwide program for awarding quarterly cash bonuses on the basis of productivity and quality. The company also has an in-house university, which offers more than 5500 free training classes from English as a second language to MBA courses.

In 1995 the U.S. Labor Department forced Solectron to pay US$237,715 in back pay to ten qualified African-American and Latino applicants who were rejected for factory and engineering jobs at the firm. In November 1999 33 Muslim employees at Solectron's manufacturing site in Suwanee, Georgia, quit after management prohibited them from taking prayer breaks. In consultation with the Council on American-Islamic Relations, Solectron agreed to rehire the employees, compensate them for lost wages, and have managers undergo religious and cultural diversity training.

Solectron is working towards implementing its California environmental standards throughout its operations worldwide. Its manufacturing facilities in France and Ireland have been awarded ISO 14001 certification.

Solectron recycles water, hazardous waste, and solid waste. It has phased out all uses of freons and volatile organic compounds in its cleaning processes for electronic circuit boards at its Milpitas, California, plant. It has formal waste reduction programs at the plant through which all business units are tracked monthly. It also recycles shipping, packaging, and soldering materials.

Solectron has placed intense emphasis on quality programs since the mid-1980s. In 1997 it won the Malcolm Baldrige National Quality Award in the manufacturing category for the second time. According to a 1998 *Industry Week* article, the company's on-time delivery rate was 99.9 percent and its in-plant defectiveness rate decreased by 63 percent in the past five years. The firm uses Japanese manufacturing techniques, including just-in-time manufacturing, total quality management, statistical process control, and continuous flow manufacturing, to achieve these goals. Line workers have the authority to shut down assembly lines if they believe quality standards are not being met.

Solectron Corp. at a Glance

Fiscal year ended: August 31
Revenue in US$ millions

	1995	1996	1997	1998	1999
Total Revenue ($)	2,065	2,817	3,694	5,288	8,391
Earnings/ Share ($)	0.2	0.27	0.34	0.41	0.56
Price to Earnings (PE)	22.86	23.31	28.47	51.06	73.173
Dividend Yield (%)	N/A	N/A	N/A	N/A	N/A

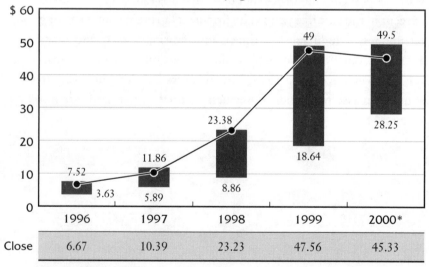

Stock Growth (High-Low-Close)

	1996	1997	1998	1999	2000*
Close	6.67	10.39	23.23	47.56	45.33

*2000 price as of August 31

40

SR TELECOM INC.

8150 TransCanada Highway
St. Laurent, PQ H4S 1M5
(514) 335-1210
www.srtelecom.com
SRX (TSE)

CEO: W. Ronald Couchman
President and COO: Pierre St-Arnaud

Community	★ ★ ★
Diversity	★ ★ ★
Employee	★ ★ ★ ★ ★
Environment	★ ★ ★
International Operations/ Human Rights	★ ★ ★
Product and Practices	★ ★ ★ ★

SR Telecom designs, manufactures, markets, installs, and services TDMA point-to-multipoint microwave and wireless loop telecommunications products and systems for use in public and private telephone and data networks. The company also implements turnkey projects for customers in 80 countries. SR Telecom primarily provides radio telephone service to rural and isolated regions worldwide where traditional wire and cable systems are not economical or reliable. Approximately 25 percent of SR Telecom's customers are industrial users. Ongoing new contracts bode well for the company, but given its historic price volatility this stock is definitely not for the faint of heart.

Although SR Telecom does not have a formal employment equity policy or any programs to encourage the hiring and promotion of women and minorities, two of its nine directors are women. This level of representation is rare in corporate Canada.

After 18 months of service, employees participate in SR Telecom's profit sharing plan. Staff with six months of continuous service are also eligible to participate in the company's employee stock purchase plan. The company supplements employee contributions (up to 5 percent of their annual salary) at levels set by a senior committee. SR Telecom also offers a variety of benefits to employees, including a tuition assistance plan. At the Montreal plant, employees can take company-sponsored French lessons.

SR Telecom undertakes environmental audits of its facilities. The company's St. Laurent and Kanata facilities are in the process of becoming certified under the ISO 14001 standard. In accordance with the guidelines of the Montreal Protocol, SR Telecom has eliminated the use of chlorofluorocarbons, which previously were an essential part of its manufacturing process. The company also has replaced ozone-depleting freon with a water-based process for its coating equipment.

Wholly owned Apollo Microwaves Ltd. has installed equipment to eliminate hazardous and toxic substances from the waste stream. SR Telecom reports that it uses no toxic chemicals in the manufacturing processes at its St. Laurent, Quebec, and Kanata, Ontario, facilities.

Many of SR Telecom's communication installations are powered by solar cells because of their remote location.

The company was awarded one of five 1997 Canadian Awards for International Development for its contract in Peru. The contract involved connecting isolated communities, scattered over an area of 250,000 square kilometres, to Peru's telephone system. SR Telecom's

Chilean subsidiary, Comunicación y Telefonía Rural S.A., has a 30-year concession to provide telephone services to nine rural zones of Chile through the operation of a local exchange carrier network.

The company's radio telecommunication products are made to operate in any climate and, regardless of location or the age of the equipment, are serviced by field staff at the company's expense.

In January 1998 SR Telecom announced that it had signed a $4.5 million contract with the Brazilian Air Force to supply its SR 500-s data and voice communication system. The value of the contract represented 2.5 percent of fiscal 1998 revenue.

SR Telecom Inc. at a Glance

Fiscal year ended: December 31

Revenue in CDN$ millions

	1995	1996	1997	1998	1999
Total Revenue ($)	143	144	169	168	193
Earnings/ Share ($)	0.41	0.13	0.3	0.09	0.2
Price to Earnings (PE)	38.41	67.91	24.33	55.83	32.86
Dividend Yield (%)	0.76	0.99	0.82	1.34	N/A

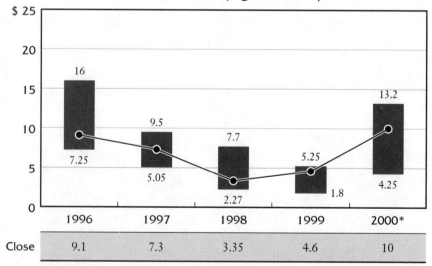

Stock Growth (High-Low-Close)

	1996	1997	1998	1999	2000*
Close	9.1	7.3	3.35	4.6	10

*2000 price as of August 31

41

STILLWATER MINING CO.

1200 Seventeenth Street
Suite 900, One Tabor Center
Denver, CO 80202
(303) 352-2060
www.stillwatermining,com
SWC (AMEX)

Chairman and CEO: William E. Nettles
President and COO: Harry C. Smith

Community	★ ★ ★
Diversity	★ ★ ★
Employee	★ ★ ★ ★
Environment	★ ★ ★ ★
International Operations/ Human Rights	★ ★ ★
Product and Practices	★ ★ ★

Stillwater Mining Company mines, processes, and refines palladium, platinum, and associated metals from a geological formation in southern Montana known as the J-M Reef. It is the only primary producer of palladium and platinum in North America. Stillwater Mining sells approximately 90 percent of its palladium and platinum production to the automobile industry for use in catalytic converters, which reduce harmful automobile emissions. Record sales of SUVs in the U.S. have contributed to demand, since SUVs require more catalysts than other automobiles. European demand for palladium has been driven by fiscal incentives for the early introduction of vehicles that meet the more stringent air emission standards that will take effect in 2003. Platinum is also used for jewellery and electrical applications such as hard disks and proton exchange membrane fuel cells for vehicles, as well as household appliances. Stillwater Mining is well positioned to meet the increasing demand for palladium and platinum worldwide.

In fiscal 1999 Stillwater Mining donated US$133,000 to charity, despite suffering pre-tax losses in 1996 and 1997. The company announced plans to contribute US$400,000 in cash and in-kind contributions to build the Rocky Mountain bighorn sheep display at ZooMontana in Billings. The area surrounding the company's mine serves as a winter range habitat for bighorn sheep.

Stillwater Mining offers paid maternity leave of six to eight weeks as part of its short-term disability benefit program. The company also offers pre-tax set-asides for medical and dependent care expenses.

Stillwater Mining grants stock options to all newly hired employees on a graded scale. For almost all of its employees, Stillwater has 401(k) savings plans through which the company matches 200 percent of employee contributions up to 3 percent of base compensation.

In January 1999 Stillwater Mining's Columbus metallurgical complex, which consists of a smelter and a base metals refinery, became the first complex ever to be twice awarded the Montana Governor's Safety and Health Achievement Award. The complex has not experienced a lost-time accident in the last five years.

Stillwater Mining does not discharge any of its nitrate-contaminated mine water into the Stillwater River, but instead recycles it for use in the mine. The company uses foxtail (a perennial plant) and operates a treatment plant that uses bacteria to reclaim nitrates created by explosives used in its mining processes. Using slope stabilization and revegetation, Stillwater has reclaimed old chrome tailings from former U.S. government-contracted mining, which ended in 1962.

Stillwater Mining has not received an environmental citation since it began operations in 1986.

In September 1999 Stillwater Mining reached a tentative agreement with Northern Plains Resource Council (NPRC) and two affiliates to resolve disagreements surrounding the expansion of the company's mine near Nye, Montana. NPRC is a grassroots citizens group dedicated to land stewardship and social justice. The "good neighbour agreement," which also includes the company's new East Boulder Mine near Big Timber, Montana, covers a variety of environmental issues, including water quality monitoring, tailings and waste rock disposal, and review of reclamation and bond coverage. Also, the parties agreed to establish a Technology and Responsible Mining Practices Committee, which will explore the research, development, and implementation of new technologies and practices related to environmental procedures and performance. As of August 2000 talks between the company and the three groups had stalled over issues of secrecy and enforceability.

Stillwater Mining Co. at a Glance

Fiscal year ended: December 31

Revenue in US$ millions

	1995	1996	1997	1998	1999
Total Revenue ($)	51	56	76	106	152
Earnings/ Share ($)	0	0.34	-0.18	0.38	0.96
Price to Earnings (PE)	–	–	–	66.67	32.2
Dividend Yield (%)	N/A	N/A	N/A	N/A	N/A

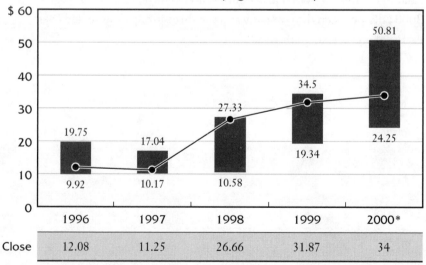

Stock Growth (High-Low-Close)

	1996	1997	1998	1999	2000*
Close	12.08	11.25	26.66	31.87	34

*2000 price as of August 31

42

SUNCOR ENERGY INC.

P.O. Box 38, 112 4th Avenue SW
Calgary, AB T2P 2V5
(403) 269-8100
www.suncor.com
SU (TSE)

President and CEO: Richard L. George

Community	★ ★ ★
Diversity	★ ★ ★ ★ ★
Employee	★ ★ ★
Environment	★ ★ ★
International Operations/ Human Rights	★ ★ ★
Product and Practices	★ ★ ★

Suncor Energy is an integrated oil and gas company. It refines, distributes, and markets conventional crude oil, heating oils, natural gas, natural gas liquids, petrochemicals, and transportation fuels; mines and upgrades oil sands in Alberta; and owns an oil shale development project in Australia. Virtually all of its growth will come from the oil sands segment. Suncor is set to double production at the oil sands plant, and possibly double it again by providing further feedstock from the nearby Firebag lease. Suncor is well positioned to benefit from strong crude oil prices.

Suncor has a policy to guide its relationship with aboriginal peoples. It provides internships and cooperative work experiences for qualified aboriginal students, organizes career fairs directed at aboriginal communities, and implements awareness programs for staff with respect to aboriginal culture and traditions. Suncor also includes aboriginal businesses in appropriate contract bidding processes. Contracts with native-owned businesses at the oil sands operation should reach $25 million in 2002.

Employees can direct the company to match their savings plan contributions in the form of company stock. Suncor has employee incentive plans through which employees are paid bonuses if corporate and/or divisional targets are achieved.

Although Suncor's lost-time injury rate compares favourably with some industry counterparts, it has experienced safety problems at the oil sands. In April 1996 the shutters of 12 nuclear gauges were left open for six days, exposing 20 maintenance workers to radiation. Suncor pleaded guilty to three counts under the *Atomic Energy Control Act* and paid fines totalling $9000. During 1998 two contractor fatalities occurred.

Suncor's environment, health, and safety committee oversees the implementation of the company's environmental policy. Outside consultants and internal staff undertake company-wide environmental assessments every three to five years, and Suncor publishes an environmental report biannually.

Suncor's Sarnia refinery recovers 35 tonnes of hydrofluoric acid per year for reuse rather than treating and discharging it into the St. Clair River. This project eliminates 110 tonnes of waste previously sent to the site's waste water discharge plant. The oil sands division conserves 2000 cubic metres of water daily by recycling waste water from the powerhouse for use in the extraction unit. A recovery basin at the oil sands has allowed Suncor to recycle 300,000 litres of waste oil per year.

Although Suncor's emissions meet regulatory limits, its substantial emissions to air and water are a significant contributor to acid rain, global warming, and smog. The oil sands operation accounts for about 70 percent of the company's overall greenhouse gas emissions. It is also the single largest source of sulphur dioxide in Alberta.

Offsets are a key component of Suncor's reduction plans. For example, in 1998 Suncor announced that it had entered into an agreement with Vision Quest Windelectric Inc. of Calgary to fund the generation of up to 350,000 kWh per year of electricity from wind turbines in Alberta. The deal is expected to result in a modest reduction of air emissions.

Suncor and its partners have constructed a demonstration plant to test the commercial and environmental viability of producing oil from an oil shale deposit in Australia. The joint venture conducted a full environmental impact assessment before beginning construction of the plant and submitted an environmental management strategy to the government. Although this process included extensive consultation with various community organizations, some environmental groups are opposed to the oil shale industry. They cite the potential for increased greenhouse gas emissions and the deposit's proximity to the Great Barrier Reef, a World Heritage Area.

Suncor Energy Inc. at a Glance

Fiscal year ended: December 31

Revenue in CDN$ millions

	1995	1996	1997	1998	1999
Total Revenue ($)	1,898	2,097	2,148	2,068	2,383
Earnings/ Share ($)	0.69	0.86	1.01	0.85	0.8
Price to Earnings (PE)	15.49	16.58	23.96	27.06	38.97
Dividend Yield (%)	2.67	2.26	1.39	1.48	1.13

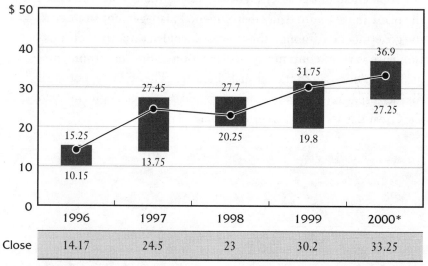

Stock Growth (High-Low-Close)

	1996	1997	1998	1999	2000*
Close	14.17	24.5	23	30.2	33.25

*2000 price as of August 31

43

TELUS CORP.

19th Floor, 3777 Kingsway
Burnaby, BC V5H 3Z7
(604) 432-2413
www.telus.com
T (TSE)

President and CEO: Darren Entwistle

Community	★ ★ ★
Diversity	★ ★ ★
Employee	★ ★ ★ ★
Environment	★ ★ ★
International Operations/ Human Rights	★ ★ ★
Product and Practices	★ ★ ★

TELUS Corporation was formed through the merger of BC Telecom and TELUS. It is the second-largest domestic Canadian telecommunications provider, and offers local and long-distance telecommunications, as well as wireless, data, and Internet access. TELUS' strategic partners include GTE Corp., which has 26 percent ownership in the company. TELUS is currently rolling out services in Ontario and Quebec to compete with Bell Canada. With national expansion plans and a healthy balance sheet, TELUS may well be the best value among the telecommunications and cable stocks.

TELUS' aboriginal relations policy acknowledges the importance of traditional aboriginal values and highlights the company's goal of creating long-term, beneficial relationships with aboriginal communities through community involvement, education, cross-cultural awareness, and employee participation.

In 1994 TELUS and the Calgary Board of Education announced Canada's first workplace school. The school, which is also open to members of the general public, runs programs for kindergarten to grade two under the auspices of the Calgary Public School Board. TELUS renovated and wired space for the school in the TELUS Calgary Tower, which the school leases.

Prior to the February 1999 merger, BC Telecom and TELUS both had employee share purchase plans. TELUS will implement a new plan for all employees. In addition, the company offers a variety of benefits, including an employee assistance plan and access to fitness facilities.

TELUS has an environmental policy and conducts both internal and external audits of its operations. Its environmental management system is designed to address specific areas such as the management and reduction of hazardous chemicals and fuel storage tanks. By 2000 TELUS intended to reduce the number of hazardous chemicals used by 50 percent of 1996 figures, and to reduce the number of fuel storage tanks to 86. TELUS also expected to reduce materials going to landfill by 30 percent of 1996 levels by 2000.

In August 1999 TELUS began renovating its Vancouver offices to improve energy efficiency, bringing energy consumption levels 35 percent below those required by city bylaws. It will incorporate recycled brick and granite into the existing building, which will be enveloped by a double-glassed shell suspended one metre from the building's face on all sides. This encasement will create a greenhouse effect, thereby reducing the need for artificial cooling in the summer and insulating the building in winter. In addition, an internal heat exchange system will divert excess heat to sections where it is needed. Recycled copper from defunct telecommunications equipment will be used to create design accents on the building. The project was expected to be complete by December 2000.

TELUS is the third-largest provider of cellular services in Canada. Despite a lack of conclusive scientific evidence, some people suspect that radio frequency (RF) and microwave radiation emitted from mobile phones and cellular towers promote serious health effects, ranging from neurodegenerative diseases to cancer. According to some reports, these radiation fields may change the body's chemical structure, affecting nerve cells and the nervous system. Health Canada's Radiation Protection Bureau's Safety Code #6, which specifies the maximum level of RF radiation to which humans may safely be exposed, states that "exposure to excessive levels of RF energy over prolonged periods can cause adverse health effects." According to the World Health Organization, mobile telephones emit RF fields that could easily exceed the current standards in light of the rapid increase in their use.

TELUS Corp. at a Glance

Fiscal year ended: December 31

Revenue in CDN$ millions

	1995	1996	1997	1998	1999
Total Revenue ($)	2,390	2,517	2,754	5,833	5,872
Earnings/ Share ($)	2	1.9	2.29	0.27	1.46
Price to Earnings (PE)	7.94	10.31	13.69	12.95	24.08
Dividend Yield (%)	13.8	11.21	7.16	7.11	3.98

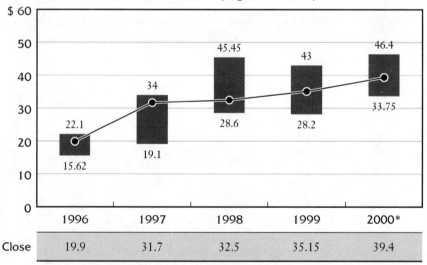

Stock Growth (High-Low-Close)

Close	19.9	31.7	32.5	35.15	39.4

*2000 price as of August 31

44

TRANSALTA CORP.

110 12th Avenue SW
Box 1900, Station M
Calgary, AB T2P 2M1
(403) 267-7110
www.transalta.com
TA (TSE)

President and CEO: Stephen G. Snyder

Community	★ ★ ★ ★
Diversity	★ ★ ★
Employee	★ ★ ★
Environment	★ ★ ★ ★
International Operations/ Human Rights	★ ★ ★
Product and Practices	★ ★ ★

TransAlta Corporation is an energy company that owns and operates 3 coal-fired generating plants and 13 hydroelectric plants in Alberta; operates 110 kilometres of distribution lines and 11,000 kilometres of transmission lines; operates co-generation plants in Canada and Australia; and trades in electricity and gas. It has been undergoing a transformation from a heavily regulated utility to a lightly regulated electricity company. Asset sales will increase profits and provide support for the dividend. TransAlta shares are underpriced and a great value for income or growth investors.

TransAlta works with aboriginal groups to increase cross-cultural awareness and employment opportunities. In 1995 the company developed an aboriginal relations policy and initiated aboriginal awareness training for its employees. It maintains an aboriginal information database that contains a skills inventory, a business inventory, and community profiles of the aboriginal communities in which the company operates. TransAlta sponsors an aboriginal scholarship program and an educational awards program.

TransAlta offers a comprehensive employee assistance program, tuition subsidies, and scholarships for employees' children. Self-directed, cross-functional work teams at TransAlta are designed to encourage employee input into decision-making and planning processes. The company's incentive pay program rewards employees for meeting predetermined individual and corporate goals. In fiscal 1999 the company provided full-time employees with 500 stock options and part-time permanent employees with 250 stock options.

TransAlta's Health and Safety Management System includes a safety policy, employee-led "Safety Challenge" steering committees (responsible for developing and implementing employee health strategies), and two auditing programs. An employee was electrocuted and killed in 1998 while inspecting a power line. Prior to this, TransAlta had not experienced a fatality in ten years.

TransAlta has an environmental policy as part of its environmental management system. The company hires external consultants to audit its facilities. Environmental management is overseen by the audit, environment, and risk management committee of the board and by various executives. TransAlta publishes an annual environmental report.

TransAlta derives approximately 14 percent of its revenue annually from its gas-fired projects. The majority of these gas-fired plants are co-generation facilities. The company also purchases power from non-fossil-fuel-based independent energy producers, including biomass, hydro, and wind-based projects in Alberta. TransAlta New Zealand operates geothermal, wind, and small hydro generating operations as well.

TransAlta has taken significant actions to reduce greenhouse gases (GHGs), fly ash, and other harmful emissions. The company participates in the federal government's Voluntary Challenge and Registry program. In a 1997 progress report, TransAlta reported a GHG intensity of 0.88 tonnes of GHG emissions per cubic metre of oil equivalent in 1996, a 12.22 percent decrease from 1990.

TransAlta derives approximately 80 percent of its energy from coal-fired power plants. These facilities produce fly ash, 99 percent of which TransAlta captures by electrostatic precipitators. The company sells the ash to cement producers for road construction, wallboard manufacturing, and other uses. The plants also emit sulphur dioxide (SO_2) and nitrous oxides, which contribute to acid rain and ground-level ozone. However, the company's emissions are well below limits established by Alberta's *Clean Air Act* and are lower than some other investor-owned utilities that use coal-fired generation. In 1998 TransAlta released approximately 2.2 grams of SO_2 per kilowatt hour of energy produced, compared to NS Power Holdings Incorporated (14 g/kWh) and Canadian Utilities Ltd. (4.5 g/kWh).

TransAlta Corp. at a Glance
Fiscal year ended: December 31
Revenue in CDN$ millions

	1995	1996	1997	1998	1999
Total Revenue ($)	1,379	1,545	1,685	1,089	1,029
Earnings/ Share ($)	1.14	1.14	1.14	1.29	1.07
Price to Earnings (PE)	12.83	15.13	22.78	20.2	27.75
Dividend Yield (%)	6.7	5.68	4.35	4.36	7.07

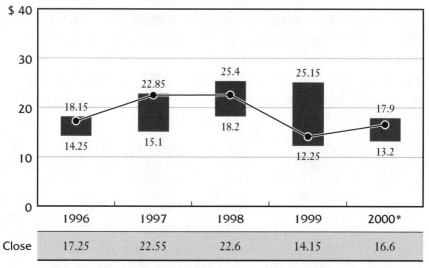

Stock Growth (High-Low-Close)

	1996	1997	1998	1999	2000*
Close	17.25	22.55	22.6	14.15	16.6

*2000 price as of August 31

45

VESTAS WIND SYSTEMS A/S

Smed Sorensens Vej 5
6950 Ringkobing
Denmark
45-96-75-25-75
www.vestas.dk
VWS (Copenhagen and London stock exchanges)

Chairman: Bent Eriit Carlsen
Managing Director: Johannes Poulsen

Community	★ ★ ★
Diversity	★ ★ ★
Employee	★ ★ ★ ★
Environment	★ ★ ★ ★
International Operations/ Human Rights	★ ★ ★
Product and Practices	★ ★ ★ ★

Vestas Wind Systems is the world's largest manufacturer of wind turbines. It has subsidiaries and joint ventures in 8 countries that service more than 7000 wind turbine sites in approximately 30 countries on 4 continents. Vestas owns its production facilities for machinery, towers, blades, and control systems, and has its own service organization. This

Danish company has developed a computerized generator system for maximum output and minimum maintenance. These modern windmills are used to create electric power. Vestas sells the windmills to power companies worldwide and has more than 20 percent of world market share.

There are two major wind companies in Denmark. We particularly like Vestas because it has grown organically rather than through acquisitions. It should benefit from the growing trend towards deregulation in the electric power industry. Since it trades on the Copenhagen Stock Exchange, you will probably have to buy this stock through a major investment firm. It is listed on the NASDAQ bulletin board, but the shares are not very liquid and you will likely pay a lot more for them. Quotes are available on the company's Web site.

None of Vestas' nine board directors or three management board members is female. Three employees of Vestas' Danish operations are members of the company's board of directors, as prescribed by Danish law.

Vestas employs almost 4500 people through its own operations, joint ventures in India and Spain, and associated companies in Denmark, Germany, the Netherlands, Sweden, and the United States. The company grew by 45 percent in 1999.

In November 1998 Vestas issued shares to its employees. As of December 1998 more than 70 percent of the eligible employees had subscribed for shares in the company. Vestas planned to undertake a similar offering in autumn 2000. Vestas employees receive extensive training. For example, when the company opened a blade factory each new employee underwent an eight-week course, supplemented with one-on-one practical training with an experienced worker.

Wind power is a zero-emission, renewable generating technology. In 1995 the wind turbine industry received support from the International Atomic Energy Agency, which stated that, all things considered, wind power would be fully competitive with fossil fuels and atomic energy by 2010. Modern wind turbines generate enough power from only 23 days of wind to balance out the amount of energy used in their production.

Vestas has an environmental policy. At its Danish operations, the company has implemented an environmental management system that complies with ISO 14001 standards. Each year Vestas develops concrete environmental goals and systematizes the collation of environmental data. The company will publish an environmental audit for the first time in connection with the release of its annual accounts for 2000. Vestas considers environmental issues in product and process development.

More than 50 employees are involved in research and development. Vestas has achieved some firsts in wind technology, including the development of lighter blades and Vestas OptiSpeed™, which allows the turbine rotor and the generator to rotate at variable speeds, thus ensuring higher energy production and lower noise levels.

Vestas has a comprehensive service network and guarantee. This network ensures that if a Vestas turbine encounters difficulties, a service team can complete the necessary service procedures within 24 hours of the error being registered—no matter where in the world the turbine is located.

Vestas Wind Systems A/S at a Glance

Fiscal year ended: December 31

Revenue in US$ millions

	1995	1996	1997	1998	1999
Total Revenue ($)	273	319	265	445	637
Earnings/ Share ($)	0.06	0.06	-0.03	0.3	0.5
Price to Earnings (PE)	–	–	–	17.87	31.6
Dividend Yield (%)	–	–	–	–	N/A

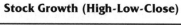

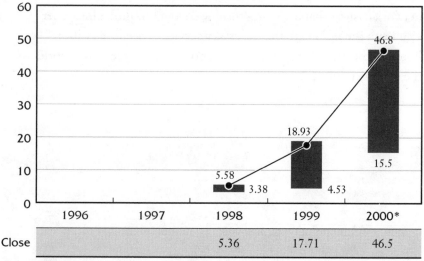

*2000 price as of August 31

*Total Revenue, Earnings per Share, and Stock Growth figures converted from Danish krone

46

WESTCOAST ENERGY INC.

1333 West Georgia Street
Vancouver, BC V6E 3K9
(604) 488-8000
www.westcoastenergy.com
W (TSE)

Chairman and CEO: Dr. Michael E.J. Phelps
President and COO: Arthur H. Willms

Community	★ ★ ★ ★
Diversity	★ ★ ★ ★
Employee	★ ★ ★
Environment	★ ★ ★
International Operations/ Human Rights	★ ★ ★
Product and Practices	★ ★ ★

Westcoast Energy is a natural gas pipeline company that gathers, processes, stores, transports, and distributes natural gas. It has operations in Canada as well as Australia and Indonesia. Three years of substantial capital spending have put downward pressure on earnings in recent years but leave Westcoast positioned to show significant earnings growth from new projects. High natural gas prices and improvements in non-regulatory energy services should also contribute to earnings. Dividend yield and long-term growth prospects make Westcoast one of the most undervalued pipeline stocks in North America.

Historically, Westcoast has supported joint ventures and business development with aboriginal communities. Since 1991, aboriginal contractors have prepared rights-of-way for all of Westcoast's pipeline gathering projects. In addition, native people contribute to the development of restoration plans following the construction of facilities. Westcoast is also integrating aboriginal peoples into environmental assessment, line location, and environmental monitoring teams.

Westcoast has a formal employment equity policy. The company offers flextime, part-time work, and flexible workweeks to help employees balance work and family responsibilities. Two of the company's 13 directors are women, a level of representation that is rare in corporate Canada.

Westcoast offers a variety of benefits, including a comprehensive employee assistance program, education grants, and retirement planning. Union Gas, a wholly owned subsidiary, maintains an on-site fitness facility (at one regional office) and programs to encourage employee health and well-being.

Westcoast's environmental, health, and safety (EHS) policy applies to all subsidiaries. The policy has a number of components, including a provision tying EHS performance to operating managers' job reviews. The Environment, Health, and Safety Council and the Health and Safety Professionals Group meet regularly and provide quarterly reports to the EHS committee of the board of directors. Westcoast publishes a sustainable development progress report annually.

Westcoast is one of Canada's largest owners and operators of cogeneration plants. It has established natural gas vehicle (NGV) systems in four provinces and provides natural gas for approximately 8000 NGVs in Canada. Although natural gas is not benign, it is the cleanest-burning fossil fuel and has traditionally been viewed as an environmentally responsible alternative to oil and coal. NGVs have demonstrated significant reductions in exhaust emissions.

Westcoast's pipeline division is the largest processor of raw natural gas in Canada, most of which is sour. During the processing of sour gas, hydrogen sulphide (H_2S) is extracted, some of which is burned at high temperatures in incinerator stacks to convert it into sulphur dioxide (SO_2), a major contributor to acid rain. The company has taken several steps to address this problem. In 1995 it implemented changes at its booster stations to minimize the flaring of liquid hydrocarbons. The company now redirects the liquids for processing, thereby reducing SO_2 emissions. Overall, the company released 11,603 tonnes of SO_2 in 1998, a 3 percent decrease from 1995.

In a 1997 report to the federal government's Voluntary Challenge and Registry program, Westcoast reported a greenhouse gas (GHG) intensity of 0.11 tonnes of GHG emissions per cubic metre of oil equivalent in 1996, a 10 percent decrease from 1990.

Westcoast has interests in power generation and/or transmission facilities in China, Indonesia, and Mexico. According to a Westcoast spokesperson, the company's activities are managed on a country-by-country basis, taking into consideration host country requirements, World Bank environmental standards, and the firm's EHS policy.

Westcoast Energy Inc. at a Glance

Fiscal year ended: December 31

Revenue in CDN$ millions

	1995	1996	1997	1998	1999
Total Revenue ($)	4,184	4,875	7,312	7,376	6,265
Earnings/ Share ($)	2.01	1.96	1.99	1.53	1.95
Price to Earnings (PE)	10.01	11.71	16.02	19.93	11.87
Dividend Yield (%)	4.62	4.58	3.64	4.13	5.53

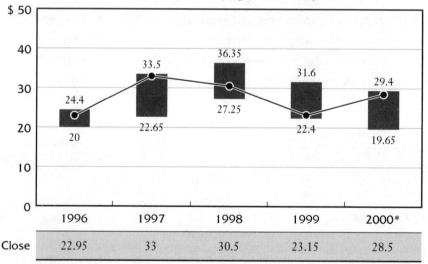

Stock Growth (High-Low-Close)

	1996	1997	1998	1999	2000*
Close	22.95	33	30.5	23.15	28.5

*2000 price as of August 31

47

WESTPORT INNOVATIONS INC.

1691 West 75th Avenue
Vancouver, BC V6P 6P2
(604) 718-2000
www.westport.com
WPT (TSE)

President and CEO: David Demers

Community	★ ★ ★
Diversity	★ ★ ★
Employee	★ ★ ★ ★
Environment	★ ★ ★ ★
International Operations/ Human Rights	★ ★ ★
Product and Practices	★ ★ ★

Westport Innovations develops fuel systems that allow diesel engines to run on natural gas, a cleaner and cheaper alternative. The company has been working with Cummins Engine, the world's largest manufacturer of diesel engines over 50 horsepower, to develop its natural gas fuelling system for heavy-duty trucks and stationary power plants. Westport has also been working with Ford Motor Co. to develop the enabling technologies for a natural gas–fuelled diesel engine for light-duty vehicles. This vehicle technology is designed to meet the low emission standards for two main diesel fuel pollutants: nitrogen oxides and particulate matter.

The new low emission standards take effect in the U.S. in 2002 and in Europe in 2003. Westport researchers are already working on solutions for even more stringent standards that will take effect in the U.S. in 2006 and 2007. Canada has also announced a national program that would meet or exceed U.S. standards. These proposed regulations would reduce the allowable sulphur content in diesel fuel and require expensive pollution abatement equipment for engines burning diesel. To meet these standards, refiners will have to increase diesel prices and engine makers will have to charge more to accommodate the cost of the pollution abatement equipment. Westport has a solution. Its technology is easy to install, drastically reduces pollutants, and actually makes trucks less expensive to operate since natural gas is much cheaper than diesel fuel. The company is simultaneously pursuing technological development in three major markets: stationary power generators, heavy-duty trucks, and light-duty vehicles.

Westport sponsors three or four scholarships per year through the federal government's National Science and Engineering Research Council (NSERC).

None of Westport's six board directors or three senior officers is female. Two of the company's eight mid-level managers are women. A Westport spokesperson reports that the company has a very diverse workforce, despite the fact that it has not implemented any formal diversity programs.

Between fiscal 1996 and fiscal 2000, Westport's workforce grew from 1 to 83 employees. As of September 2000 it employed 110 people, none of whom is unionized. The company offers stock options to all employees after six months of service. It has an employee assistance program and provides shower and change facilities for staff members who cycle to work. Westport supports the continuing education of its employees, offering time off and 100 percent reimbursement for tuition and books.

In a December 1999 study conducted for the Canadian government, entitled Alternative and Future Fuels and Energy Sources for Road Vehicles, Westport's HPDI (high-pressure direct-injection) technology was recognized as the most cost-effective solution (of those investigated) for reducing greenhouse gas emissions from heavy-duty diesel trucks.

Westport Innovations Inc. at a Glance

Fiscal year ended: December 31

Revenue in CDN$ millions

	1995	1996	1997	1998	1999
Total Revenue ($)	N/A	N/A	N/A	N/A	N/A
Earnings/ Share ($)	-0.01	-0.06	-0.16	-0.26	-0.35
Price to Earnings (PE)	N/A	N/A	N/A	N/A	N/A
Dividend Yield (%)	N/A	N/A	N/A	N/A	N/A

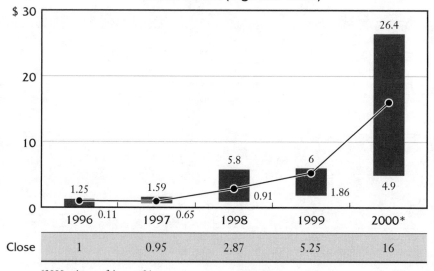

Stock Growth (High-Low-Close)

| Close | 1 | 0.95 | 2.87 | 5.25 | 16 |

*2000 price as of August 31

48

WHOLE FOODS MARKET INC.

Suite 300, 601 North Lamar Boulevard
Austin, TX 78703
(512) 477-4455
www.wholefoods.com
WFMI (NASDAQ)

Chairman, CEO, and Co-Founder: John Mackey
President: Chris Hitt

Community	★ ★ ★
Diversity	★ ★ ★ ★ ★
Employee	★ ★ ★ ★
Environment	★ ★ ★ ★
International Operations/ Human Rights	★ ★ ★
Product and Practices	★ ★ ★ ★

Whole Foods Market, Inc. owns and operates natural foods supermarkets under the names Whole Foods Market, Fresh Fields, Bread and Circus, Wellspring Grocery, and Merchant of Vino. It is the largest U.S. chain of natural foods supermarkets, with 112 stores in 22 states and the District of Columbia. *Fortune* reported that Whole Foods is the twenty-sixth-largest food and drug company in the U.S. Whole Foods stores carry extensive lines of organic produce and minimally processed products and feature "green" departments that carry environmentally safe and recycled household products. The company actively seeks out and supports artisan food producers, organic farmers, and small batch producers. It recently merged its nutritional supplements and Internet divisions into a new subsidiary called WholePeople.com. Whole Foods and Gaiam, Inc. recently merged their Internet properties into Gaiam.com, Inc.

Whole Foods contributes a minimum 5 percent of after-tax earnings in cash and goods to charity each year. The company makes charitable contributions primarily at the store level so it can assist local community groups. It offers employees 20 hours of paid time off per year for community service.

One of six senior line executives is female. Two women serve on the company's nine-member board of directors. This level of diversity at the senior management and board levels is rare in corporate America. In 1993 Whole Foods set specific goals and established incentives for team leaders to increase employee diversity to match the demographics within a five-kilometre radius of each store.

Whole Foods has gain sharing programs for which approximately 90 percent of its employees are eligible. The programs award cash bonuses to teams that meet sales, productivity, and financial goals. Whole Foods has also made stock options available to all employees. It awards options based on the employee's position and tenure with the company.

Whole Foods regards its employees as team members, and employees operating in up to nine teams run stores. These department teams make decisions relating to hiring, purchasing, pricing, and marketing. Teams are responsible for meeting productivity and financial goals.

Whole Foods also has an open book policy under which employees have access to key financial information, including sales reports and labour and company balance sheets. The company also makes available a wage disclosure report listing the gross pay earned by each team member, including executives.

Whole Foods' employees are not organized under collective agreements. Unions argue that the company's employees receive hourly wages below the norm and that it deliberately hires younger workers to forestall unionizing efforts. Union members have picketed some stores.

Whole Foods has set a high quality standard for its products, including foods that are free of artificial sweeteners, colours, flavours, and preservatives; meats free of growth hormones, antibiotics, and other chemicals; and grain products that have not been bleached or bromated. In December 1999 the company announced plans to ban genetically modified ingredients from its private label products, which accounted for approximately 12 percent of 1999 sales. Stores will not carry cosmetic, household, or other products that have been tested on animals.

Whole Foods limits the maximum compensation of any employee to ten times the average compensation of all full-time employees. In fiscal 1998 the company's CEO received a compensation package estimated at US$490,000, notably low among companies followed by Kinder, Lydenberg, Domini & Co., Inc., an American social investment research firm.

Whole Foods Market Inc. at a Glance

Fiscal year ended: September 30

Revenue in US$ millions

	1995	1996	1997	1998	1999
Total Revenue ($)	496	946	1,117	1,389	1,567
Earnings/ Share ($)	0.58	-0.53	1.06	1.64	1.54
Price to Earnings (PE)	33.84	56.25	42.96	27.96	26.5
Dividend Yield (%)	N/A	N/A	N/A	N/A	N/A

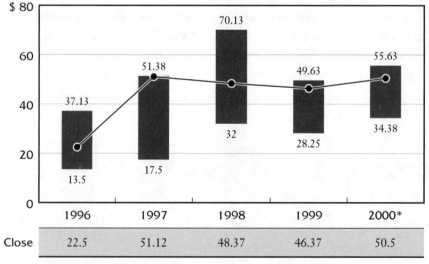

Stock Growth (High-Low-Close)

	1996	1997	1998	1999	2000*
Close	22.5	51.12	48.37	46.37	50.5

*2000 price as of August 31

49

XEROX CORP.

P.O. Box 1600, 800 Long Ridge Road
Stamford, CT 06904
(203) 968-3000
www.xerox.com
XRX (NYSE)

Chairman and CEO: Paul A. Allaire
President and COO: Anne M. Mulcahy

Community	★ ★ ★ ★
Diversity	★ ★ ★ ★ ★
Employee	★ ★ ★ ★ ★
Environment	★ ★ ★ ★ ★
International Operations/ Human Rights	★ ★ ★
Product and Practices	★ ★

Xerox Corporation develops, manufactures, markets, services, and finances copiers, electronic printers, and other office and computer equipment. Through its subsidiaries it provides network management, consulting, design, and integration services. Xerox should benefit from an ongoing shift from copiers to digital, multi-function products and network solutions in the global document market. Xerox has strong brand recognition and a broad product line to support future earnings growth.

Through Xerox's Social Service Leave program, selected employees can spend one year working for a community organization of their choice. Employees apply for the program and are selected by their peers. As of 1999, more than 450 employees have participated in this program.

Xerox's president and COO, one of five senior line executives, is female. Three women and one minority member serve on the company's 14-member board of directors. This level of diversity at the senior management and board levels is rare in corporate America.

Xerox offers family leave of 13 weeks (one week longer than required by legislation), phaseback for new mothers, resource and referral services, and adoption aid of US$3000. It also offers a US$10,000 lifetime stipend ($2000 per year) for child care, subsidized backup care at five locations, pre-tax set-asides, and direct child-care subsidies. In addition, it has an elder-care program. Telecommuting, job sharing, flextime, and compressed work weeks help staff balance their work and family responsibilities.

Xerox has a cash profit sharing program and an employee stock ownership plan in which most domestic employees can participate. It sets aside approximately 10 percent of its management bonus pool to reward outstanding performance in areas such as personal values, style, or interaction with other employees. The company fosters employee development and a work environment that encourages employee empowerment.

Approximately 6 percent of Xerox's employees are represented by labour unions, and the company has forged a strong partnership with its primary union. Xerox shares all financial and operating information with employees on cost-saving teams and allows employees to serve as equal members on work teams.

Xerox has established company-wide environmental management systems. Its major manufacturing sites worldwide are ISO 14001 certified. Xerox publishes a comprehensive annual environmental report and monitors the environmental records of its suppliers.

Xerox has established a goal to create waste-free products within waste-free factories and offices. This initiative targets nine areas, including air emissions, solid and hazardous wastes, water emissions, energy conservation, and use of post-consumer materials. In 1998, 88 percent of non-hazardous wastes were reused or recycled, leading to savings of US$45 million. The company beneficially managed 94 percent of hazardous waste through recycling, treatment, or fuels blending, an improvement of 2 percent from 1997. Equipment remanufacture or reuse/recycling diverted more than 65.8 million kilograms of waste from landfill in 1998.

In 1992 Xerox introduced copiers with recyclable cartridges. Customers can mail used cartridges, toner containers, and some varieties of used toner to Xerox at the company's expense. Xerox then recovers and reprocesses residual toner and reuses or recycles used cartridges and toner containers. In 1998 the company diverted nearly 4.3 million kilograms of additional waste from landfills as a result.

The company's Document Center 265 digital copier, introduced in 1997, allows key parts to be removed and easily remanufactured. It is 97 percent recyclable and 80 percent remanufacturable.

In fiscal 1998 Xerox's CEO received a compensation package valued at US$17.56 million, including a non-cash component consisting primarily of stock options valued at US$7.04 million. The CEO received compensation of US$32.92 million in 1997.

As we go to press in late October, Xerox continues to face problems in its transition from a copier company to a document company. It has announced its first quarterly loss in 16 years and cut its dividend by 75%. Xerox has some serious restructuring challenges ahead. It may even have to sell off part of its fabled Palo Alto Research Center, the birthplace of such technology basics as the computer mouse. Though its share price has plummeted as a result, we will watch with great interest how a large corporation with exceptional social and environmental strengths deals with these bottom line issues in the months ahead.

Xerox Corp. at a Glance

Fiscal year ended: December 31

Revenue in US$ millions

	1995	1996	1997	1998	1999
Total Revenue ($)	16,588	17,378	18,144	19,447	19,228
Earnings/ Share ($)	-0.88	1.66	2.02	0.52	1.96
Price to Earnings (PE)	13.42	15.85	18.29	25.27	11.46
Dividend Yield (%)	2.19	2.2	1.73	1.22	3.53

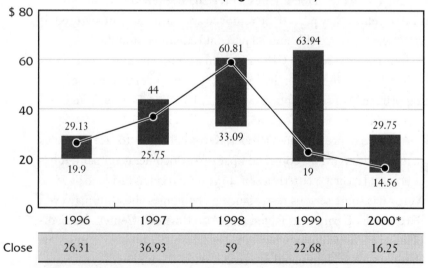

Stock Growth (High-Low-Close)

	1996	1997	1998	1999	2000*
Close	26.31	36.93	59	22.68	16.25

*2000 price as of August 31

50

ZENON
ENVIRONMENTAL INC.

3239 Dundas Street West
Oakville, ON L6M 4B2
www.zenonenv.com
ZEN (TSE)

Chairman and CEO: Dr. Andrew Benedek

Community	★ ★ ★
Diversity	★ ★ ★
Employee	★ ★ ★ ★ ★
Environment	★ ★ ★ ★
International Operations/ Human Rights	★ ★ ★
Product and Practices	★ ★

ZENON Environmental manufactures membrane-based products
for water purification and designs, builds, sells, and leases sanitary
waste water systems. It markets its mobile water purification unit to
developing countries and regions with limited freshwater supplies or
contaminated sources. Given the number of contracts it has won,
ZENON's technology seems to be gaining wider acceptance. It is

pursuing business opportunities in a number of market segments worldwide. ZENON should be able to profit from increased infrastructure spending as concern about water quality becomes more prevalent in North America and Europe.

In 1998 ZENON completed a microfiltration-based drinking-water plant for the Temagami First Nation of Bear Island, Ontario. ZENON donated the plant, which will ensure a safe supply of drinking water, to the community of 200 residents. In 1999 ZENON donated a manually transportable water filtration unit to Uganda. Canadian Physicians for Aid and Relief transported the unit to displaced people in compounds throughout the northern regions of Uganda.

ZENON has formal employment equity and sexual harassment policies. The company posts job positions in agencies, such as the Regional Indian Friends Centre, that specialize in the recruitment of disadvantaged groups.

All permanent ZENON employees are eligible to participate in the company's incentive compensation plan. Payments, which are made in cash and ZENON stock, are based on the company's return on assets and the employee's salary, job level, and performance review. Employees may also purchase ZENON shares through a payroll deduction program, under which the company matches employee contributions. It has implemented a share option plan for all employees.

ZENON has a formal environmental policy and environmental management systems. The company conducts regular audits of its facilities. An environmental committee, comprising a corporate environmental officer and divisional representatives, is responsible for implementing programs and employee training.

ZENON derives 100 percent of its revenue from the sale of products that incorporate a proprietary membrane technology that separates particles and impurities from water without the need for harmful chemicals. The technology has a variety of applications, including water purification, process separation, recycling and recovery, and waste water treatment. Treated water can be discharged to groundwater, used for irrigation, or recycled for cleaning purposes.

ZENON's water purification and waste water treatment products range in size from those handling less than five litres of liquid daily (designed for research laboratories) to those handling over 4.5 million litres daily (large industrial systems). For example, ZENON constructed a system to treat waste water at a General Motors plant in Windsor and has installed a permanent membrane-based drinking water treatment plant in Collingwood, Ontario. In February 1999 ZENON received a contract from the Olivenhain Water District near San Diego to build the largest ultrafiltration drinking-water plant in North America.

In 1994 ZENON installed a mobile water purification system at a Rwandan refugee camp that purified 40,000 litres of polluted, cholera-laden water each day.

In July 1998 the company completed an offering of non-voting Class A shares, which have the same rights and are equal to the company's common shares, except with respect to voting rights. The non-voting Class A shares will automatically convert into common shares on June 10, 2008.

ZENON Environmental at a Glance

Fiscal year ended: December 31

Revenue in CDN$ millions

	1995	1996	1997	1998	1999
Total Revenue ($)	40	53	58	77	98
Earnings/ Share ($)	-0.51	0.08	0.09	0.23	0.1
Price to Earnings (PE)	–	98	79.17	57.61	109.09
Dividend Yield (%)	N/A	N/A	N/A	N/A	N/A

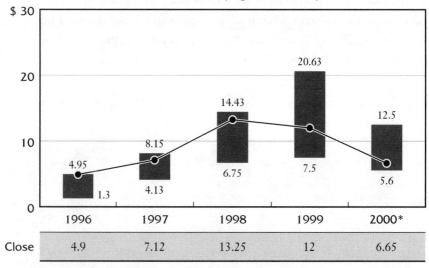

Stock Growth (High-Low-Close)

Close	4.9	7.12	13.25	12	6.65

*2000 price as of August 31

THE BEST ETHICAL STOCKS RANKED
BY SCREENING CRITERIA* AND BY
TOTAL POINTS SCORED

Top Five Community Companies:

1. Polaroid Corp (5, 24)
2. Fannie Mae (5, 23)
3. Xerox Corp (4, 24)
4. The Bank of Nova Scotia (4, 23)
5. *Tie:* Bank of Montreal, Hewlett Packard, Husky Injection, Investor's Group, Nokia (4, 22)

Top Five Diversity Companies:

1. *Tie:* Polaroid Corp, Xerox Corp (5, 24)
2. *Tie:* Fannie Mae, The Bank of Nova Scotia, Intel Corporation, Whole Foods Inc. (5, 23)

Top Five Employee Companies:

1. Xerox Corp (5, 24)
2. Intel Corp (5, 23)
3. *Tie:* Noranda Inc., Husky Injection (5, 22)
4. *Tie:* Cisco Systems, SR Telecom Inc. (5, 21)

Top Five Environment Companies:

1. *Tie:* Xerox Corp, Polaroid Corp (5, 24)
2. Intel Corp (5, 23)
3. Interface Inc. (5, 22)
4. *Tie:* Nortel Networks, Electrolux (5, 21)

Top International Operations / Human Rights Companies:

1. The Bank of Nova Scotia (4, 23)
2. Nokia (4, 22)

Top Five Products & Practices Companies:

1. *Tie:* Whole Foods, Fannie Mae (4, 23)
2. *Tie:* Investor's Group, Bank of Montreal (4, 22)
3. *Tie:* Electrolux, Vestas Wind Systems, SR Telecom, Solectron Corp (4, 21)

---

* The first number refers to the company's screening criteria score; the second to its total score.

INDEX

CANADIAN BUSINESS
for SOCIAL RESPONSIBILITY

"In 1998 Michael Russo and Paul Fouts examined the performance of 243 Fortune 500 companies over a two year period. Their research found that companies with superior environmental performance (preventing pollution at the source) had higher returns on investment compared to their competitors. The companies tended to be more innovative, conserving valuable resources and enhancing their reputation for both prospective employees and customers. As socially responsible investors we must consider the social and environmental impacts of our investments. Deb Abbey and Michael Jantzi are giving us the tools we need to make investment choices that reflect our values. By investing with our values, we can help build a just and sustainable economy."

Debra Elliot
President
Canadian Business for Social Responsibility

CBSR is an organization that promotes, supports and educates about socially and environmentally responsible business practices that benefit employees, the community and the economy.

To find out more about CBSR check out cbsr.bc.ca or call 1-604-323-2714.

To join, send in this form and receive a 10% discount.

Company Name:	
Company Contact:	
Position/Title:	
Mailing Address:	
Postal Code:	
Telephone:Fax:	
E-mail:	
No. of employees:	

(Full-time equivalent)

Type of Membership: ☐ Member   ☐ Sustaining Member

☐ I consent to the use of my name or my business's/company's name in CBSR promotional material.

Declaration:
I declare that I support the principles of Canadian Business for Social Responsibility (CBSR).

Look for these other titles in

the 50 BEST

for CANADIANS series

The 50 Best Stocks for Canadians
Philip Benson and Gene Walden
ISBN 0-7715-7708-7

Blue-chip stocks are a fundamental part of any investment portfolio, and this book highlights the best of the best.

The 50 Best Stocks Under $20 for Canadians
Philip Benson and Gene Walden
ISBN 0-7715-7706-0

The ultimate guide to Canadian small-cap stocks! They won't be under $20 for long...

The 50 Best Internet Stocks for Canadians:
Long Term Investing in the Internet Economy
Mark Pavan, Gene Walden, and Tom Shaughnessy
ISBN 0-7715-7721-4

Don't get burned with an unlucky guess... use this book to learn more about investing in Internet stocks, and see which companies have outperformed their peers.